A NOTE TO PARENTS AND TEACHERS

Smithsonian Readers were created for children who are just starting on the amazing road to reading. These engaging books support the acquisition of reading skills, encourage children to learn about the world around them, and help to foster a lifelong love of books. These high-interest informational texts contain fascinating, real-world content designed to appeal to beginning readers. This early access to high-quality books provides an essential reading foundation that students will rely on throughout their school career.

The four levels in the Smithsonian Readers series target different stages of learning abilities. Each child is unique; age or grade level does not determine a particular reading level. See the inside back cover for complete descriptions of each reading level.

When sharing a book with beginning readers, read in short stretches, pausing often to talk about the pictures. Have younger children turn the pages and point to the pictures and familiar words. And be sure to reread favorite parts. As children become more independent readers, encourage them to share the ideas they are reading about and to discuss ideas and questions they have. Learning practice can be further extended with the quizzes after each title and the included fact cards.

There is no right or wrong way to share books with children. You are setting a pattern of enjoying and exploring books that will set a literacy foundation for their entire school career. Find time to read with your child, and pass on the amazing world of literacy.

Adria F. Klein, Ph.D.
Professor Emeritus
California State University San Bernardino

Smithsonian

READERS

Endless Explorations

LEVEL 4

World Wonders

Predators

Space Exploration

Natural Disasters

Ocean Habitats

Flight

Silver Dolphin Books
An imprint of Printers Row Publishing Group
10350 Barnes Canyon Road, Suite 100, San Diego CA 92121
www.silverdolphinbooks.com

ISBN 978-1-62686-454-2
Manufactured, printed, and assembled in Dongguan City, China
19 18 17 16 15   1 2 3 4 5

Predators written by Brenda Scott Royce
Space Exploration and Flight written by Stephen Binns
Natural Disasters and Ocean Habitats written by Emily Rose Oachs
World Wonders written by Kaitlyn DiPerna
Edited by Kaitlyn DiPerna
Editorial Assistance by Courtney Acampora
Cover and Book Design by Jenna Riggs
Cover Production by Rusty von Dyl

Predators, Natural Disasters, and Ocean Habitats reviewed by Dr. Don E. Wilson,
        Curator Emeritus of the Department of Vertebrate Zoology,
        National Museum of Natural History, Smithsonian
Space Exploration reviewed by Andrew K. Johnston, Geographer for the Center for
        Earth and Planetary Studies, National Air and Space Museum, Smithsonian
World Wonders and The Science and History of Flight reviewed by
        F. Robert van der Linden, chairman of the Aeronautics Division, National Air
        and Space Museum, Smithsonian

For Smithsonian Enterprises:
Kealy Gordon, Product Development Manager, Licensing
Ellen Nanney, Licensing Manager
Brigid Ferraro, Vice President, Education and Consumer Products
Carol LeBlanc, Senior Vice President, Education and Consumer Products
Chris Liedel, President

HOW TO USE THIS BOOK

Glossary

As you read each title, you will see words in **bold letters**. More information about these words can be found in the glossary at the end of each title.

Quizzes

Multiple-choice quizzes are included at the end of each title. Use these quizzes to check your understanding of the topic. Answers are printed at the end of the quiz, or you can reread the title to check your answers.

Fact Cards

Each title comes with six tear-out fact cards. Read the cards for fun or use them as quizzes with a friend or family member. You'll be impressed with all you can learn!

ABOUT THE SMITHSONIAN

Founded in 1846, the Smithsonian is the world's largest museum and research complex, consisting of 19 museums and galleries, the National Zoological Park, and nine research facilities. The Smithsonian's vision is to shape the future by preserving our heritage, discovering new knowledge, and sharing our resources with the world.

SMITHSONIAN READER SERIES

Level 1 Early Adventures

Animal Habitats

Outer Space

Reptiles

Vehicles

Safari Animals

Insects

Level 2 Seriously Amazing

Nighttime Animals

Sea Life

Dinosaurs and Other Prehistoric Creatures

Solar System

Baby Animals

Human Body

Level 3 World of Wonder

Sharks!

Wild Weather

Rain Forest Animals

The United States

The Planets

Ancient Egypt

Level 4 Endless Explorations

Predators

Space Exploration

Natural Disasters

World Wonders

Ocean Habitats

The Science and History of Flight

CONTENTS

☀ Smithsonian

PREDATORS

Brenda Scott Royce

CONTENTS

WHAT IS A PREDATOR?

Predators inspire fear and fascination. We tend to think of them as bloodthirsty beasts with powerful jaws and razor-sharp claws. But not all predators are large, aggressive animals.

A predator is any animal that hunts another animal for food. Predators range in size from giant killer whales to tiny tree frogs. They may be **solitary** or social, speedy or slow-moving.

Predators are born with hunting skills according to their environment and their **prey**. Some predators chase their prey. Other predators hide and wait for their prey to come to them.

One thing all predators have in common: they must kill in order to survive.

Predators are a natural and necessary part of every food chain. A food chain is a series of living things in which the next lower member is used as a source of food. Important nutrients and energy are passed to each animal or plant in a food chain.

A food chain starts with plants, which get their energy from sunlight. Herbivores (plant-eating animals) get energy from eating the plants. Carnivores (meat-eating animals) get their energy from eating other animals. Omnivores eat both plants and animals for energy.

All of the overlapping food chains in an **ecosystem** make up a food web.

Healthy ecosystems depend on balanced food chains. If one animal's food source disappears, the other animals in the food chain will be affected. Overhunting, overfishing, pollution, and habitat destruction can all disrupt a food chain.

Some animals are both predator and prey. While these animals are hunting for food, they must also be on the lookout for larger animals seeking to attack them.

The kit fox is a desert predator. It eats rodents, rabbits, lizards, and large insects. These small foxes are on the menu for several larger predators—especially coyotes.

Armadillos are predators, primarily feeding on ants and termites. Armadillos are preyed upon by wild cats and birds of prey. The three-banded armadillo's thick shell and its ability to curl into a tight ball protect it from most enemies. But a jaguar's powerful jaws can pierce through this body armor.

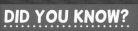

? DID YOU KNOW?

In a healthy ecosystem, prey will always outnumber predators.

An animal at the top of its food chain is called an **apex predator**. Once fully grown, these animals have no natural enemies other than humans. African lions, killer whales, and saltwater crocodiles are examples of apex predators.

Polar bears are the top predators of the Arctic region. They hunt for seals and other marine mammals by waiting near breathing holes in the ice. When a seal surfaces, the polar bear pounces, striking out with its huge paws and sharp claws.

The Bengal tiger hunts a wide variety of prey—including deer, wild boar, water buffalo, and even crocodiles. No other animal hunts the tiger.

The gray wolf is top dog in any ecosystem it inhabits. Gray wolves prey on many different animals, including elk, deer, and moose. Where their habitat overlaps with coyotes or cougars, gray wolves out-compete these rivals for food.

fossa

The island of Madagascar is two hundred and fifty miles away from mainland Africa. The island's top predator—the fossa—faces no competition from lions or cheetahs. A relative of the mongoose, the fossa has retractable claws that can come out like a cat's claws. These claws help the fossa as it climbs swiftly through trees in pursuit of its favorite food: lemurs.

lemur

BUILT TO KILL

Predators are born with features that enable them to hunt. Some are equipped with fangs or stingers for delivering a deadly dose of **venom**. Sharp teeth or beaks allow predators to tear apart flesh. Claws slash and stab, disabling prey or perhaps striking the fatal blow.

Like most cats, lions have retractable claws which extend like switchblades when it's time to attack. A lion's tongue is rough like sandpaper, which helps the cat rip apart meat. Female lions do most of the hunting (and caring for cubs), while males defend the pride.

The octopus has eight legs with which to catch prey, but those incredible limbs are not its deadliest weapons. A sharp beak helps the octopus break through the shells of clams and other sea creatures, and venomous saliva paralyzes or kills prey.

Scorpions have a stinger at the tip of their tail, which they use to inject venom into their prey.

A grizzly bear uses its sharp claws to fish for salmon.

The African wild dog uses its large teeth like scissors to rip apart flesh and crush bone. Also known as painted dogs, these skilled hunters primarily prey on antelope.

Super long and lightning fast, the chameleon's tongue is a marvelous tool for catching insects! It has a sticky tip that forms a small suction cup when it strikes its target. Once it snags its prey, the chameleon pulls its tongue back into its mouth as quickly as it was extended.

The boa constrictor uses its entire body as a weapon, wrapping around its prey and slowly squeezing the air from its lungs.

Sharp senses help predators detect prey. Speed and **agility** come in handy when chasing or stalking. Strength is a major asset in making the kill. These are just some of the skills predators use to get the job done.

The cheetah—the fastest land mammal—can chase down prey at speeds of up to 70 miles per hour.

Owls have keen eyesight and great hearing—traits that make them excellent hunters.

In addition to the same five senses humans possess (sight, smell, hearing, taste, and touch), sharks have a sixth sense: they can detect the electrical impulses given off by other animals in the water. This sense helps sharks locate fish hiding nearby.

Just as predators are born with skills for hunting and killing, their prey are born with skills to avoid being hunted and killed. Some are fast runners, and some zigzag when they run. Some have coloring that **camouflages** them and helps them hide. Some simply taste bad or are poisonous to eat.

Predators have many different ways of capturing prey. The alligator snapping turtle tricks its prey, using its own tongue as bait! Sitting with its mouth wide open, the turtle flails its pink tongue around like a worm, hoping to lure a hungry fish.

Most predators approach their prey as quietly as possible. They creep, they crouch, they scurry, they slither, or they stalk . . . silently searching for the best angle to attack.

Ambush predators are masters of surprise. Rather than chasing their prey, they hide and wait for prey to come to them. Crocodiles lurk in the water with just their eyes and nostrils above water. When an animal approaches the water to drink, the crocodile lunges out of the water and snaps its powerful jaws around its prey.

The praying mantis blends in with green leaves. When it spots its prey, the mantis springs into action, grasping the victim with its spiked legs and eating it alive—and often headfirst.

Some animals team up to take down prey. Hunting in a group is generally more successful than hunting alone, as prey can more easily escape from a single predator.

A group of hyenas can hunt larger prey than a single hyena could hope to overpower on its own. Jackals will take turns tiring out a fleeing gazelle.

Killer whales, or orcas, usually hunt in family groups, called pods, of up to 40 other orcas. The pod works together to surround a school of fish, and then slap their strong tails against their prey. This stuns the fish, which the orcas then eat.

OVER ACHIEVERS

Most predators are content to pick on prey smaller than themselves. But some have their eyes on a bigger prize. These over achievers are capable of catching or consuming prey larger than themselves.

Mountain lions are solitary hunters. Their diet includes deer, elk, and bighorn sheep. Killing these large mammals requires considerable skill and stealth. When a mountain lion moves in for the kill, it usually bites the back of the neck.

Thanks to extremely flexible jaws and an expanding throat, the egg-eating snake can swallow an egg much larger than its own head. Bony projections in the snake's esophagus break the eggshell. The snake digests the yummy contents of the egg and spits up the crushed shell.

Komodo dragons can kill prey as large as water buffalo! These fearless lizards are bold enough to pursue animals several times their size. Water buffalo often manage to escape the initial attack, but shock and blood loss—perhaps quickened by venom in the dragon's bite—prove overwhelming.

Officially declared the world's most venomous spider, Brazilian wandering spiders often eat frogs, mice, lizards, and birds.

Birds of prey—also known as raptors—share many characteristics that make them great hunters: forward-facing eyes, sharp talons (claws), and hooked beaks. This group of animals includes eagles, hawks, falcons, and owls. Most raptors catch their prey with their talons—sometimes in mid-air—a task requiring excellent eyesight and rapid reflexes.

Birds of prey usually attack from behind to minimize the chance of being seen. An owl's downy feathers allow it to fly silently— adding to the element of surprise.

Harpy eagles' talons are bigger than a grizzly bear's claws! One of the largest and most powerful eagle species, harpy eagles can snatch monkeys and sloths right out of the tree tops.

Osprey are also known as "fish hawks" because of their skill at catching live fish. These large birds often hover briefly over the water before diving—feet first—to grab a fish. The osprey then carries its catch in its talons back to its nest or perch.

Not all predatory birds are classified as raptors. As their name suggests, kingfishers are great at catching fish—but they also eat frogs and lizards, snatching them up in their long, thick bills.

Herons can stand completely still in shallow water for more than an hour waiting for prey (mostly fish and frogs) to come within reach.

Although commonly called "killer whales," orcas are actually the largest member of the dolphin family. They are fierce predators that use their 4-inch long teeth to slice through their prey.

When piranhas close their mouths, the triangular teeth fit together like a zipper! These fish rarely waste energy attacking healthy prey, preferring to go after weak and injured creatures. The presence of blood in the water can result in a "feeding frenzy" in which a school of piranha strips all the flesh off an animal within minutes.

One of the deadliest predators in the ocean could fit in the palm of your hand! The blue-ringed octopus is about the size of a golf ball. Its venom is thousands of times stronger than cyanide, which can kill humans in only minutes.

The great white shark is the largest predatory fish. Built for speed, these sharks can swim up to 35 miles per hour. The great white shark has up to 300 teeth in its mouth at one time, arranged in rows. Large marine mammals like dolphins and seals are no match for these toothy terrors.

Emperor penguins dive deep below the ocean's surface to catch fish, which they swallow whole. The penguin has barbs on its tongue to prevent slippery fish from escaping.

DESERT PREDATORS

Desert dwellers have to be resourceful. Only the toughest animals can survive in areas where food and water are hard to come by.

Coyotes are very adaptable animals. They adjust their hunting style depending on what food is available. Coyotes will team up to hunt deer, but for smaller prey they prefer going solo. These omnivores will eat just about anything, including cactus fruit and flowers.

Rattlesnakes have folding fangs that swing into striking position when they open their mouth wide. Heat-sensing pits on each side of their head help rattlesnakes find warm-blooded prey. Most rattlers strike quickly and then release their victim. They wait nearby for the venom to take effect.

? DID YOU KNOW?

When threatened, rattlesnakes hiss and rattle their tails to frighten intruders. But the rattle is not used in hunting, when a silent approach works best.

Roadrunners seldom fly; they run across the desert in pursuit of food. These brave birds seize scorpions by the tail and don't shy away from attacking snakes. They typically batter their prey, smashing it against the ground or a rock.

Like many desert animals, the shrew can survive without drinking water. It gets the moisture it needs from its prey. Desert shrews eat insects, spiders, lizards, and even scorpions.

The desert tarantula has two large fangs for injecting venom. The venom turns its prey's insides into a soupy mush. These spiders eat insects, lizards, other spiders, and small animals.

JUNGLE PREDATORS

Found mainly in Central and South America, jaguars prefer large prey, including deer, hogs, and even small crocodiles. They are good climbers and will often ambush their prey by leaping down from trees.

? DID YOU KNOW?

The name jaguar comes from a Native American word that means "beast who kills with one leap."

The tree frog's color helps it blend in with tree leaves. It hides on a leaf waiting for insects to approach then snatches them with a quick flick of its sticky tongue. Crickets, moths, flies, and other insects are the tree frog's main prey, but they've also been known to eat other small frogs.

At up to 550 pounds, the anaconda is the world's largest snake. This massive serpent makes its home in the South American tropics, where it eats wild pigs, deer, birds, large rodents, fish, and reptiles. Anacondas constrict their prey, squeezing until the animal can't breathe. Loosely hinged jaws allow anacondas to swallow their prey whole—no matter the size.

PREDATOR PLANTS

There are more than 720 carnivorous plant species on the planet. Most live in areas where there are few nutrients in the soil. Most get their energy by consuming insects (some also eat small lizards, frogs, and other animals). These predators cannot chase their prey. They must wait for prey to wander into their trap.

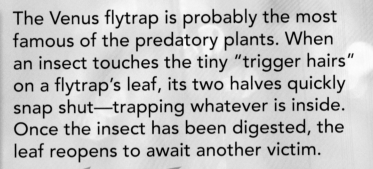

The Venus flytrap is probably the most famous of the predatory plants. When an insect touches the tiny "trigger hairs" on a flytrap's leaf, its two halves quickly snap shut—trapping whatever is inside. Once the insect has been digested, the leaf reopens to await another victim.

Insects attracted to the glistening leaves of the butterwort are in for a sticky surprise! The plant's leaves are coated in a greasy liquid that traps bugs. When a bug struggles to escape, the plant produces even more slime. Enzymes in the slime begin to break down the bug so that its nutrients can be absorbed by the plant.

 DID YOU KNOW?

Bugs aren't the only thing on the menu for these predators. Carnivorous plants have been known to consume frogs, lizards, small rodents, fish, and—in rare cases—birds.

Specialist predators eat only one type of prey. As its name suggests, the snail kite (a type of hawk) dines only on snails. Australia's fat-tailed gecko is a termite specialist, and will often go hungry rather than settle for a different bug. On the other side, **opportunistic predators** will eat nearly any animal they can catch.

Blue whales have one thing on their minds at suppertime— krill! These huge whales eat by taking in huge mouthfuls of water and straining it through their jaw. Thousands of krill (tiny shrimplike creatures) are left behind for the whale to swallow.

Survival is tougher for specialists. The more varied an animal's menu, the more options it has at dinnertime. Black-footed ferrets eat prairie dogs— and almost nothing else. So when prairie dog colonies began to disappear, the black-footed ferret was in big trouble! In 1986, there were fewer than 20 black-footed ferrets left on the planet. Conservation efforts have helped increase their numbers, but black-footed ferrets are still **endangered**.

We know that predators have special skills that make them great hunters. But how do predators acquire these amazing abilities? Many young predators learn through play. Play provides practice for real situations, allowing young animals to challenge themselves. For a kitten, stalking and pouncing on a sibling is great fun—and educational!

During play fights, animals are careful not to hurt one another. Tiger cubs may bite, but not hard enough to cause an injury. These play sessions help the cubs gain strength and speed.

Wolf pups learn to handle competition by play-fighting with other members of the pack. Play also helps wolves establish bonds of friendship, which are important for pack animals.

Another way animals learn is through observation. Sea otters learn their hunting skills by carefully watching the actions of role models—usually their mothers. In addition to learning how to hunt, young predators must learn which animals make good prey.

Some animal mothers are great teachers. Cheetah mothers often release injured prey to give their cubs the opportunity to make the kill. Of course, the prey animal may escape from the inexperienced cub. But improving the cub's hunting skills—and increasing its odds of survival—are worth the risk.

VIPs:
VERY IMPORTANT PREDATORS

Predators play a vital role in keeping ecosystems healthy. The disappearance of a predator can lead to disastrous changes for the animals that share its habitat.

Consider the case of California's Channel Islands. A change in predators was disastrous for the island's ecosystem. Bald eagles and island foxes had lived together on the Channel Islands for thousands of years. The eagles, which preyed mostly on fish, were not interested in eating the foxes. Things changed when bald eagles began disappearing from the islands in the 1960s, mainly due to **pesticide** poisoning.

With no more bald eagles on the island, a new predator moved in: the golden eagle. But unlike the bald eagles, golden eagles found the island foxes to be very appetizing. In less than 10 years, golden eagles killed 95 percent of the foxes!

Today, biologists are working to restore the natural balance on the Channel Islands, making them once again safe for the island fox.

People are predators, too. Humans are omnivores; we eat both plant and animal foods. We are at the top of many food chains.

Many predators need our protection. Snow leopards live in the mountains of central Asia, where they are an apex predator. Though nothing preys on snow leopards, their numbers are declining. Threats to the snow leopard include habitat loss, illegal hunting, and reduction of available prey. They are one of several large carnivores currently classified as endangered.

People often take pity on prey animals and view predators as "bad guys." But to keep our ecosystems healthy and balanced, we need them both.

PREDATORS QUIZ

1. **What is a predator?**

   a) Any animal eaten by another animal
   b) Any mammal that eats animals
   c) Any animal that hunts another animal for food
   d) Any large, aggressive animal

2. **Who gets their energy from eating only plants?**

   a) Carnivore
   b) Herbivore
   c) Predator
   d) Omnivore

3. **What is the top predator in Madagascar?**

   a) The Bengal tiger
   b) The lemur
   c) The cheetah
   d) The fossa

4. **What is an ambush predator?**

   a) A predator that waits for prey to come to them
   b) A predator that chases prey
   c) A predator that hunts in groups
   d) A predator that swims

5. **Which does NOT kill prey larger than itself?**

   a) Mountain lion
   b) Orca
   c) Komodo dragon
   d) Brazilian wandering spider

6. **Which is NOT a raptor?**

   a) Eagle
   b) Owl
   c) Kingfisher
   d) Hawk

7. **What animal family do killer whales belong to?**

   a) Orca family
   b) Fish family
   c) Shark family
   d) Dolphin family

8. **What animal's name means "beast who kills with one leap"?**

   a) Jaguar
   b) Hyena
   c) Fossa
   d) Leopard

Answers: 1) c 2) b 3) d 4) a 5) b 6) c 7) d 8) a

GLOSSARY

Agility the ability to move quickly and easily

Ambush predators predators that hide and wait for prey

Apex predator an animal at the top of its food chain

Camouflages blends in with surroundings

Ecosystem a community of all the living things in an area

Endangered at risk of becoming extinct

Opportunistic predators predators that will eat whatever food is available

Pesticide a poison used to kill pests such as insects

Prey an animal that is hunted and killed by another animal for food

Solitary alone

Specialist predators predators that eat only one type of prey

Venom a poison produced by animals such as snakes, spiders, and scorpions and usually injected by biting or stinging

POLAR BEAR

KILLER WHALE

GRAY WOLF

TIGER

HARPY EAGLE

TARANTULA

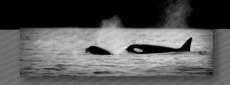

Favorite Foods: seals, sea lions, sharks, whales
Weight: up to 22,000 pounds
Orcas will tip over ice floes to send seals and penguins toppling into the water.

Favorite Food: seals
Weight: up to 1,500 pounds
A polar bear's paw measures about 12 inches across.

Favorite Foods: deer and wild pigs
Weight: 220 to 660 pounds
A tiger's bite is almost twice as strong as a lion's!

Favorite Foods: deer, elk, moose
Weight: 35 to 130 pounds
Hunting in a pack, wolves can take down prey up to 10 times their size.

Favorite Foods: insects, frogs, mice
Weight: 1 to 3 ounces
The largest tarantula, the goliath bird-eating spider, is about the size of a dinner plate.

Favorite Foods: sloths, snakes, lizards, monkeys
Weight: 10 to 20 pounds
Harpy eagles chase prey through the rain forest at up to 50 miles per hour.

SPACE EXPLORATION

Stephen Binns

CONTENTS

DREAMS OF OUTER SPACE

Are your daydreams about outer space sometimes wild and even bizarre?

You are not alone. You are in very good company.

Most of the great pioneers of space flight were world-class daydreamers. Before a leap into space, there must come a great leap of the imagination.

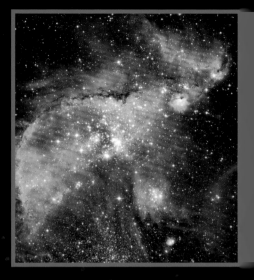

Ursa Minor

Our exploration of space, in fact, began as a great nighttime daydream. We looked to the stars and imagined the patterns that we call **constellations**.

Do you ever look to the stars and wonder: Are we alone here on Earth?

Well, as you will see

STORIES IN THE SKY

Ancient people everywhere stared into the night sky and saw constellations. By connecting stars with imaginary lines, people could form pictures of animals and gods in the night sky. Entire stories were created around these constellations.

Lion

Hercules

The Romans saw a constellation of a lion, the fierce enemy of their god and hero Hercules. They also saw a constellation of a crab, that battled with Hercules. But the crab didn't fare too well—Hercules simply stepped on him. Hercules, too, had his own constellation.

Ancient people watched the night sky almost as if it were television. The stars of the show were actually stars!

Constellations are nothing more than a romantic idea. The stars in constellations have no real connection to each other. But **astronomers** still use constellations to create a map of space.

The ancient Greek astronomer Ptolemy (TOL-ah-me) identified forty-eight constellations. Modern astronomy has added forty more. Modern constellations are also named for creatures they look like.

It has gone this way through the history of our exploration of space. Science and dreaming work hand in hand.

"I think it's part of the nature of man to start with romance and build to reality," said the science fiction writer Ray Bradbury. "In order to get the facts, we have to be excited to go out and get them."

One of the great space explorers was a man who never left Italy, the place of his birth. Galileo Galilei was the first astronomer to use a telescope to study the sky. He was teaching the ideas of Ptolemy at the time. When he looked through the telescope, he saw that much of what he was teaching was not true.

Ptolemy thought that everything in the sky moved around the Earth. Galileo, through his telescope, saw four moons moving around Jupiter.

To Ptolemy, other planets, like Jupiter, could not have moons revolving around them.

Galileo saw something different. He saw proof that Earth is not the center of it all.

In 1989, the U.S. space agency NASA sent a space probe to the planet Jupiter. A space probe is a spacecraft without people aboard. The craft was named *Galileo*. It studied the four moons that Galileo had seen through his telescope 400 years earlier.

Galileo spacecraft

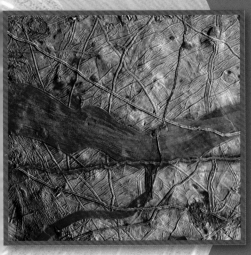
image of Europa taken by Galileo spacecraft

Galileo the astronomer saw the four moons only as four points of light. *Galileo* the spacecraft saw the moons as four worlds.

One of the moons, Europa, held a special surprise. This moon is covered in ice cracked into blocks. Below the blocks may be an ocean of water. Where there is water, there may be life.

? DID YOU KNOW?

At the end of the mission, NASA sent Galileo crashing into Jupiter. Otherwise, it might have disturbed whatever life forms may be on Europa.

THE FIRST MARTIANS

Galileo discovered that Earth is not the center of the **universe**. With this discovery came another idea. Maybe we are not alone in the universe.

In 1877, the Italian astronomer Giovanni Schiaparelli turned his telescope to the planet Mars. He saw a curious thing. On the surface of Mars he thought he saw long, straight lines. Writing of what he saw, he used the Italian word canali to describe the lines.

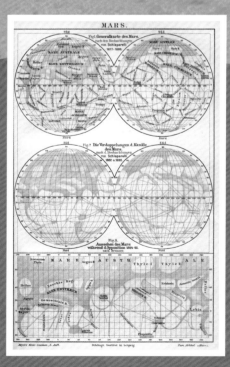

In Italian, canali can mean any channels of water. But when the astronomer's report came out in English, the word canali became the word it most looks like: canals.

A "canal" can mean only one thing in English. A canal, like the Panama Canal, is a channel of water that was built by someone.

In the United States, astronomer Percival Lowell looked through his own telescope for the Martian canals. Sure enough, there they were!

Percival Lowell wrote books about the very intelligent Martians who had built the canals. The British science fiction writer H. G. Wells soon wrote *War of the Worlds*, in which the very intelligent Martians invade the Earth.

artist's impression of the surface of Mars

The canals turned out to be a trick of the eyes. Sometimes our eyes see a jumble of faraway things as something very tidy, like a straight line. In Percival Lowell's case, the trick of the eyes might have been helped along by wishful thinking.

THE ROCKET AND THE CHERRY TREE

The novel *War of the Worlds* came out in the United States in 1898. One of the readers was a Massachusetts teenager named Robert Goddard. The story stayed with him for a long time.

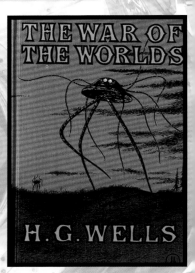

One year later, Robert climbed a cherry tree in his family's orchard to trim its branches. He would remember the date of this simple chore for the rest of his life: October 19, 1899.

Mars

While sitting in the tree, Robert looked to the sky and thought about Mars.

When he climbed down from the tree, he later said, he was "a different boy" from when he climbed up.

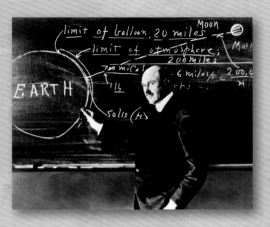

That day, Robert began his life's work—to find a way of leaving our planet.

He came up with ideas of how to fire a rocket to outer space. He sent his ideas to the Smithsonian in Washington, D.C. The Smithsonian sent money to help his research.

One idea was to use a liquid fuel, such as gasoline, as the rocket's **propellant**. In 1926, he fired off the world's first liquid-fuel rocket from his aunt's farm in Massachusetts.

He knew that a rocket would need a lot of fuel to reach space. The fuel would weigh the rocket down. He got the idea of a rocket in sections, each section holding fuel. The sections would break away when the fuel was used up.

These ideas would help carry men to the Moon and space probes to Mars.

ROCKET SCIENCE MADE EASY

If you have a balloon handy, you can easily launch your own small-scale rocket.

First, blow up the balloon. Now pinch the opening to keep the air in. Now let go and watch the balloon fly.

When the opening was closed, the pressure inside the balloon was pushing out with the same force in all directions.

When you let go, the pressure near the opening escaped. The pressure near the top of the balloon was still strong. This stronger pressure propelled the balloon forward.

You noticed, of course, that your balloon rocket did not fly all the way to outer space.

That's the hard part of rocket science!

Your balloon rocket used air as its propellant. The rockets that got us to the Moon used a million gallons of burning fuel.

capsule

boosters

A thing that is shot into space is tiny compared to the "booster," the parts of the rocket that hold the fuel.

The Moon rocket, the Saturn 5, stood 363 feet tall. The three **astronauts** were squeezed into a capsule on the tip of the rocket. Imagine the capsule as the little cap on a jumbo-sized tube of toothpaste. The rocket is the tube.

second stage

The Saturn 5 was a "three-stage rocket." Each stage carried fuel. Each stage broke off and fell away when the heavy fuel was used up. This left only the little toothpaste cap to carry the astronauts to the Moon.

German bomber over London

Robert Goddard was not the world's only rocket scientist. German scientists also developed rockets. During World War II, Germany shot more than a thousand rockets, called V-2s, to bomb cities, especially London.

The United States and the Soviet Union were **allies** in defeating Nazi Germany in 1945. The two nations came out of the war as the world's two "superpowers." Both sides captured V-2 rockets to study them. Each nation brought German scientists to its side to work on new rocket projects.

V-2 rocket at the Smithsonian

The United States and the Soviet Union were soon in a "cold war." The nations were enemies but the guns and the rocket weapons were not fired. There were other ways to do battle. The battle for space was called the "space race."

The space race was not a sprint. It was a marathon that lasted twenty years. For much of the time, there was no clear finish line. Even so, the U.S. was trailing behind at the start.

In 1961, President John F. Kennedy announced a clear goal and a deadline for the United States: "landing a man on the Moon and returning him safely to the Earth" by the end of the decade.

In the Space Race, the Soviets took the first lead. In October 1957, a Soviet two-stage rocket launched *Sputnik 1*, the world's first **artificial satellite**. It orbited Earth for three months before falling and burning in the **atmosphere**.

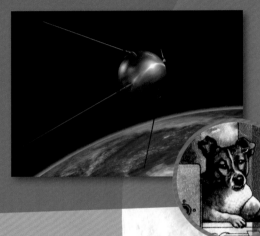

In November 1957, the Soviets followed with *Sputnik 2*. This satellite carried the first earthling into **orbit**: a stray dog named Laika.

The United States sent up its first satellite, *Explorer 1*, in January 1958. That year, the U.S. Congress created the National Aeronautics and Space Administration (NASA).

In May 1959, NASA sent two monkeys into space, Able and Baker. The monkeys did make it safely back to Earth, but they had not reached orbit.

America's animals, too, were trailing behind.

Able and Baker

Both sides were working toward sending a human into space. In January 1961, NASA sent the next best thing: a chimpanzee named Ham.

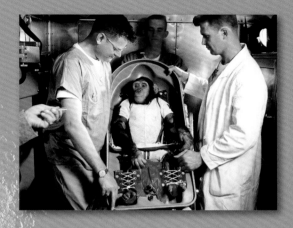

Three months later, a Soviet cosmonaut (the name for a Soviet astronaut) became the first human to fly into space. He also entered Earth's orbit. The young cosmonaut, Yuri Gagarin, (YOO-ree ga-GARE-in) circled the Earth in 108 minutes.

NASA sent its first astronaut to space the next month. Astronaut Alan Shepard flew 116 miles above Earth in the capsule *Freedom 7*. He was gone for 15 minutes.

NASA's advance to the Moon came in three steps, or projects, each one with a name from **myth**.

Project Mercury was named for the messenger god. In 1962, Mercury finally sent an astronaut into orbit. John Glenn circled the Earth three times. He saw three sunrises and three sunsets and returned in five hours!

Project Gemini, named for twins in myth, launched the first two-man missions. In 1965, Gemini astronaut Ed White became the first American to take a "walk" in the zero **gravity** of space. This was practice for walking on the low-gravity Moon.

Project Apollo was named for the god of light. It would end at the Moon, but the first mission never left the ground. A fire in the capsule of Apollo 1 killed astronauts Ed White, Gus Grissom, and Roger Chaffee.

The first mission to the Moon, Apollo 8 was only supposed to make a test in Earth's orbit. But U.S. officials learned that the Soviets were at work on their own Moon project. In August 1968, NASA asked the Apollo 8 astronauts if they'd like to go to the Moon instead by the end of the year.

Apollo 8 did not land on the Moon, but it entered the Moon's orbit. Astronauts Jim Lovell, Frank Borman, and Bill Anders were the first people to look upon the far side of the Moon, the side that is always turned away from Earth.

But the astronauts' eyes kept turning to another sight. There in the sky, the Moon's sky, was an "earthrise," like the rising of the Moon as seen from Earth.

 **DID YOU KNOW?**

On Christmas Eve 1968, astronaut Frank Borman sent a television greeting to everyone back on Earth. It was the largest audience ever to hear a human voice.

Though no one planned for this, the contest between the U.S. and the Soviet Union was becoming something very different. The whole world was paying attention.

Reaching the Moon would be a milestone for all human beings.

The Apollo 11 mission landed on the Moon before President Kennedy's deadline, on August 20, 1969.

President Kennedy did not live to see it. He was assassinated while riding in a parade in Dallas, Texas, in 1963.

Apollo 11 used a lunar module to land on the Moon. Think again of the rocket as a tube of toothpaste. The cap on the tube is the astronauts' command module.

The astronauts' lunar module was attached to the top of command module. The lunar module rode through space, upside-down, on the top of the tube of toothpaste.

The lunar module separated from the command module in the Moon's orbit. Astronaut Michael Collins stayed in the command module, circling the Moon. Astronauts Neil Armstrong and Buzz Aldrin landed on the Moon on the lunar module's bug-like legs.

lunar module landing and blasting off

To get off the Moon, the two would have to blast off in the lunar module and hook up again with the command module in the Moon's orbit.

Neil Armstrong was the first to step off the lunar module and into the dust of the Moon. Without knowing for sure if he would ever return to Earth, he spoke the famous words:

"That's one small step for a man, one giant leap for mankind."

Buzz Aldrin stepping onto the Moon

MOVING ON

Neil Armstrong might have changed the order of his words and the words would have been just as true. He might have said: "That's one giant leap for a man, one small step for mankind."

The courage and effort and intelligence it took to take that step added up to something gigantic. But a trip to the Moon is the tiniest of steps when we look at the whole of space—or even the whole of our solar system.

The Moon is 240,000 miles away. The trip to the Moon took four days.

The unmanned space probe *Voyager 2* began a trip in 1977. It traveled 3 billion miles to pass the planet Neptune before flying out of the solar system. The trip to Neptune took 12 years.

In the 1970s, the Cold War was pausing—at least in space. In 1972, the United States and the Soviet Union agreed to work together on a space mission. An Apollo capsule and a Soviet Soyuz capsule linked up in Earth's orbit. The old enemies were shaking hands up there!

Both sides were finding ways to keep people in space for a longer time, but closer to home, in Earth's orbit.

In 1971, the Soviet Union put into orbit the world's first space station, Salyut 1. A space station is a place where people can live and work comfortably in space.

The U.S. quickly followed with the Space Shuttle Program. Space shuttles were winged orbiters launched from rockets. They shuttled astronauts to and from space stations and space telescopes.

MAKING MARS OURS

We went to the Moon because it was the place we could reach. But we never let go of the old dreams of Mars.

In 1971, the space probe *Mariner 9* entered the Martian orbit. It discovered valleys and channels on Mars that seemed shaped by ancient floods. Mars is a very cold, very dry desert. But if there was once water on Mars, there may have once been life.

In 2004, the robot rovers *Spirit* and *Opportunity* began a long crawl over the surface of Mars. One of their discoveries gave us new hope. Mars, in fact, once held water—right there on its surface.

Since the 1970s, there has been serious talk of making a new home for humans on Mars.

Although large numbers of humans will not be living on Mars any time soon, some people have proposed remarkable plans.

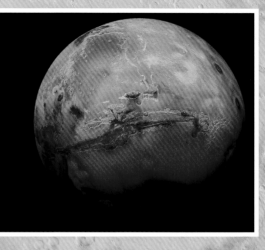

NASA scientist Christopher McKay had an idea of pumping **greenhouse gases** into the Martian atmosphere. This might warm things up.

A British scientist had an idea of setting off atomic bombs on Mars. The bombs might release water below the Martian surface. This might give Mars a nice misty atmosphere.

The British scientist's name, by the way, was Martyn Fogg!

The most exciting things in space are now being discovered using Galileo's old device, the telescope.

Telescopes use lenses or mirrors to make faraway objects seem near. The bigger the telescope, the more light it collects. The more light it collects, the better we can see.

And the farther away we are from the light and air of Earth, the better we can see light in space.

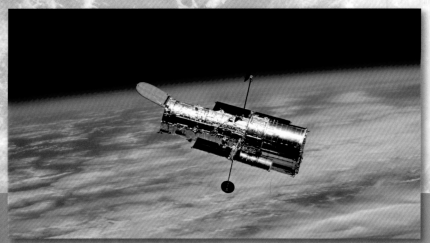

In 1990, NASA launched the Hubble Space Telescope from the space shuttle *Discovery*. Hubble travels in Earth's orbit, far away from our light and air. Hubble has given us the clearest views of the farthest galaxies.

In 1995, astronomers made the first telescope discovery of a planet outside of our solar system—a planet circling a star other than our Sun. Since then, hundreds of other planets have been discovered. The hunt is now on for Earth-like planets—planets that can support life.

Is there a chance of finding life like us, someone we can talk to?

"Let's say there is a planet like ours around the star closest to our Sun," says Smithsonian planet hunter Lisa Kaltenegger. "You send out a signal that says, 'Hi, who are you?' Four years later, your signal arrives. Another four years later, the answer arrives. And you are really happy, because you had eight years to come up with a better question!"

It will be difficult, in other words. But, says Lisa, "we've got a lot to discover and so much more to learn."

By looking at the farthest galaxies, we can look far back in time, nearly to the time when the universe began. How can that be?

A telescope sees light. Light takes time to travel. Light travels at a speed of 6 trillion miles a year. That is called a light-year.

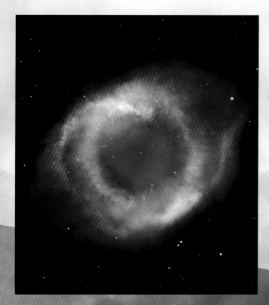

The star closest to our Sun is 4 light-years away. What we see is the light that began its journey from the star four years ago.

The Hubble Space Telescope has shown us galaxies more than 10 billion light-years away. The light began its journey 10 billion years ago!

A telescope is a time machine. To look out in space is to look back in time.

Imagine that right now you are on a planet revolving around a star that is 400 light-years away. Let's say that you have a very powerful alien telescope.

Point the telescope toward planet Earth.

The Earth you are seeing is not the Earth of today. It is the Earth 400 years ago.

Turn the telescope to Europe, then focus on Italy. Try to find the Leaning Tower of Pisa.

There it is!

Galileo is somewhere in Pisa.

Maybe he is looking through his telescope, studying, and maybe wishing on your star!

SPACE EXPLORATION QUIZ

1. **Which was discovered by Galileo?**

   a) Craters on the Moon
   b) Rings around Saturn
   c) Moons orbiting Jupiter
   d) Mountains on Mars

2. **Who built the world's first liquid-fuel rocket?**

   a) Robert Goddard
   b) Percival Lowell
   c) H. G. Wells
   d) Giovanni Schiaparelli

3. **What was the name of the world's first artificial satellite?**

   a) *Explorer 1*
   b) Laika
   c) *Sputnik 1*
   d) *Sputnik 2*

4. **What does NASA stand for?**

   a) National Aeronautics and Space Agency
   b) National Air and Space Association
   c) National Aeronautics and Space Administration
   d) National American Space Agency

5. Who was the first human to fly into space?

a) Yuri Gagarin
b) Neil Armstrong
c) Buzz Aldrin
d) Alan Shepard

6. How long did it take Apollo 11 to get to the Moon?

a) Two hours
b) Four days
c) Three months
d) Six days

7. What space probe discovered valleys and channels on Mars?

a) *Voyager 2*
b) *Salyut 1*
c) *Mariner 9*
d) *Apollo 11*

8. What is the Hubble?

a) A space probe
b) A lunar rover
c) A space shuttle
d) A space telescope

Answers: 1) c 2) a 3) c 4) c 5) a 6) b 7) c 8) d

GLOSSARY

Allies people or nations joined together for a common purpose

Artificial satellite an orbiting machine used to collect and send information

Astronauts someone who is trained to travel in spacecraft

Astronomers scientists who study stars, planets, comets, and asteroids

Atmosphere the mass of gases surrounding a planet or moon

Constellations a particular or recognizable pattern of a group of stars

Gravity the force of attraction between objects that depends on their mass

Ursa Minor

Greenhouse gases gases that keep the Sun's warmth trapped in a planet's atmosphere

Myth a story used to explain mysteries in nature

Orbit the path of a planet, moon, comet, or spacecraft around another body, such as a planet, moon, or star

Propellant the fuel that drives a rocket forward

Universe all the space, matter, and energy in existence

HUBBLE SPACE TELESCOPE

LUNAR MODULE

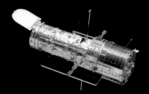

MARS ROVER

MERCURY CAPSULE FRIENDSHIP 7

MERCURY CHIMPANZEE CAPSULE

SATURN 5 ROCKET

Size: 23 feet high
Launched: 1969

"The *Eagle* has landed!" said Neil Armstrong when landing on the Moon. *Eagle* was the name of the lunar module.

Size: 43 feet long
Launched: 1990

The Hubble Space Telescope circles the Earth 14 or 15 times a day.

Size: 9½ feet high
Launched: 1962

John Glenn took three spins around Earth in this cramped capsule. On the ride, he ate applesauce to see if people can eat in space. (We can.)

Size: 5 feet long
Launched: 2003

The rovers Spirit and Opportunity, two "robot geologists," discovered signs of past water on Mars.

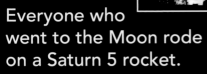

Size: 363 feet high
Launched: 1968

Everyone who went to the Moon rode on a Saturn 5 rocket.

Size: 40 inches high
Launched: 1961

During spaceflight, American chimps ate dried banana pellets as a reward for completing tasks.

Smithsonian

NATURAL DISASTERS

Emily Rose Oachs

CONTENTS

WHAT IS A
NATURAL DISASTER?

Whether a whirling tornado or raging wildfire, a natural disaster occurs from violent forces of nature. Natural disasters can cause millions of dollars in damage, put lives in danger, and even change Earth's natural landscape.

Scientists try to predict when the next natural disaster will hit. They can warn people of approaching tornadoes, hurricanes, and thunderstorms. But some natural disasters are more difficult to predict. Volcano eruptions, earthquakes, and tsunamis can appear suddenly and with little warning.

Natural disasters may be devastating for humans. But some are actually good for the environment. Wildfires bring regrowth to forests. Volcanoes create new land. Floods leave behind nutrient-filled soil. These disasters are part of Earth's natural cycle.

EARTHQUAKES:
SERIOUS SHAKERS

Many massive slabs of rock on the Earth's crust fit together like puzzle pieces. Each of these pieces is called a **tectonic plate**. Tectonic plates are constantly in motion. They shift, slide, and bump into each other. The movement of the plates against each other causes the earth to shake violently, creating earthquakes.

More than 50,000 earthquakes occur each year. Most earthquakes last for less than a minute. Many can barely be felt. But more intense earthquakes may trigger landslides, tsunamis, volcanic eruptions, and other natural disasters.

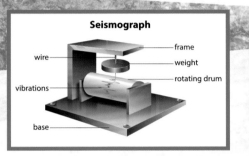

An earthquake feels stronger the closer you are to its epicenter. The epicenter is the point on the Earth's surface at the center of the earthquake. A large earthquake may be felt hundreds of miles away from its epicenter.

Seismograph

- frame
- wire
- weight
- vibrations
- rotating drum
- base

Scientists measure the intensity, or magnitude, of an earthquake. They use the Richter scale to rate the earthquake's power from 1 to 10. Magnitude 1 earthquakes are very weak. All earthquakes measured at 5 or higher are considered destructive.

SAN FRANCISCO, 1906

In 1906, a magnitude 7.8 earthquake struck San Francisco, California. Flames engulfed the city after the earthquake. Fires burned up 28,000 buildings in San Francisco.

TSUNAMIS:
WALLS OF WAVES

A tsunami is a series of gigantic waves, called a wave train. A tsunami can be caused by an earthquake, volcano eruption, landslide, or even a meteor crashing into the ocean.

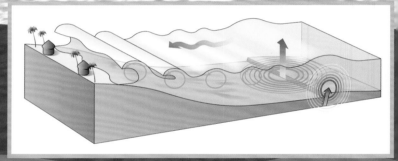

Tsunami waves speed through deep ocean water at over 500 miles per hour. They can travel across an ocean in just a few hours.

A tsunami slows down as it reaches the coast. The bottom of the wave moves more slowly than the top. This pushes the wave up to extreme heights. When it reaches land, tsunamis may tower 100 feet over the shore!

Before the first wave hits, the ocean water sometimes pulls back from the coast. This leaves the seafloor exposed for hundreds of feet. The first wave usually strikes shortly after the ocean pulls back.

A tsunami's mighty waves surge over land. They may push hundreds of feet inland. The waves sweep away buildings, trees, and anything else that stands in their path.

INDIAN OCEAN TSUNAMI, 2004

In December 2004, a tsunami occurred in the Indian Ocean. A magnitude 9.1 underwater earthquake triggered the waves. In some places, the tsunami waves grew to be over 50 feet tall. The waves' force destroyed entire villages. The tsunami ruined roads, communication systems, buildings, and homes.

VIOLENT VOLCANOES

A volcano is a vent in the Earth's crust that erupts ash, lava, and gases into the air. Volcanoes usually look like dome-shaped or cone-shaped mountains. Lava and ash build up over many years to create these mountains.

Beneath the Earth's crust is the **mantle**. The mantle is so hot that it melts rock. The melted rock moves up toward the Earth's surface. The liquid rock flows out of a volcano as lava!

All volcanoes erupt differently. Some have thin lava that spills down their sides. Others shoot lava powerfully into the air. Some explode violently, spewing gas and gray ash.

Over 1,500 **active volcanoes** dot the Earth's surface.
About 75 percent of these are in the Ring of Fire
in the Pacific Ocean. The Ring of Fire is formed by
the boundaries of tectonic plates. Like earthquakes,
volcanoes usually form where plates bump against
each other.

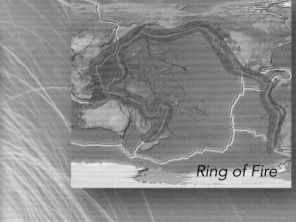

Ring of Fire

Volcanoes may trigger avalanches or tsunamis.
Their lava flows may threaten cities, roads, and homes.
But volcanoes are very important to the planet.
They created 80 percent of the Earth's surface!

KRAKATOA, 1883

In 1883, Indonesia's volcano
Krakatoa violently erupted.
Thick clouds of ash reached
50 miles high. The dust and
ash blocked sunlight around
the world. This lowered
Earth's temperatures the year
after the eruption.

TERRIBLE THUNDERSTORMS

A thunderstorm is a rainstorm with thunder and lightning. Some intense thunderstorms also bring frozen rain called hail and gusty winds.

Thunderstorms form when warm, moist air rises into the **atmosphere**. As the air goes higher, it rapidly cools. Tiny water droplets form tall, fluffy thunderclouds. Eventually, the water droplets fall back to Earth as rain.

Ice and water droplets collide in the clouds, creating electricity. Lightning bolts form to get rid of the electricity's energy. The heat from the lightning causes the air around it to vibrate. Thunder's rumbles and cracks come from this vibration.

Supercell thunderstorms are the most powerful type of thunderstorm. These intense storms can drop hail the size of grapefruits. Their winds may blast at 100 miles per hour. Supercell thunderstorms often turn into violent, destructive tornadoes.

MID-ATLANTIC DERECHO, 2012

In June 2012, a string of intense thunderstorms sped across 700 miles of the Eastern United States. This line of windy thunderstorms is known as a derecho. Winds faster than 80 miles per hour were recorded. The storms downed power lines and tore roofs off houses. About 4 million people were left without power.

A tornado is a violent windstorm with a spinning, funnel-shaped cloud. This strong storm has the power to destroy anything in its path.

All tornadoes come from thunderstorms. But not all thunderstorms turn into tornadoes. The most violent tornadoes develop from powerful supercell thunderstorms.

A thunderstorm forms when rapidly rising air cools. This cool air becomes thunderclouds. A tornado forms when the air rises even faster. The wind inside the cloud starts to whirl around. The whirling creates a column of air that spins at high speeds. The column stretches from the cloud to the ground.

On the ground, the wild winds
can cause a great deal of damage.
Tornadoes suck in dust, rubble,
garbage, and trees. The strongest
tornadoes can demolish houses or
move semi-trailer trucks!

More tornadoes occur in
Tornado Alley than anywhere
else in the world. Tornado Alley
is an area in the central United
States. About 1,000 tornadoes
happen in the United States
each year. Most of those
happen in Tornado Alley.

TRI-STATE TORNADO, 1925

*The 1925 Tri-State Tornado is among the most destructive
tornadoes in U.S. history. It traveled 219 miles across
Missouri, Illinois, and Indiana. Towns were completely
crushed, and 695 people were killed in the storm.*

HURRICANES:
TROPICAL TORMENTS

A hurricane is a massive, swirling tropical storm. When it strikes land, it brings powerful winds, heavy rain, and tall waves. Hurricanes are most common in late summer and early fall.

A hurricane forms in tropical waters that are warmer than 80 degrees Fahrenheit. This warm water **evaporates** quickly into the air and forms clouds. Wind and the Earth's rotation make these clouds swirl. As the clouds increase in speed, the storm develops into a hurricane. They can grow to almost 600 miles across!

Winds spin around the hurricane's center, called the eye. With no clouds, wind, or rain, the eye is the calm in the middle of the storm.

When hurricanes strike land, they devastate the coast. Their clouds can drop more than 2.4 trillion gallons of rain in one day. Winds may reach speeds of over 160 miles per hour. These forceful winds knock over trees and tear roofs off houses. Giant mounds of waves, called storm surges, crash on shore and flood coastlines.

? DID YOU KNOW?

A hurricane relies on warm ocean water for energy. The storm dies out when it reaches cold water or travels inland.

HURRICANE KATRINA, 2005

In August 2005, Hurricane Katrina struck states along the Gulf Coast. In New Orleans, Louisiana, 10 inches of rain and huge storm surges caused widespread flooding. Within days of the storm, 80 percent of the city was underwater.

FLOODS:
DEEP WATERS

Across the world, floods are the most common weather-related disasters. They happen when water covers land that is typically dry.

Floods usually occur when heavy rain falls for a long period of time. Rivers or lakes spill onto surrounding land because they can't handle the extra water.

Sometimes floods happen with little or no warning. These are flash floods, and they can be very dangerous. Small streams may turn into raging rivers after only a few hours of intense rain.

Coastal flooding occurs along the seashore. Massive waves and huge storms draw surging seawater onto shore.

? DID YOU KNOW?

Moving water can be extremely destructive. Only six inches of rushing water can knock down a person. Just two feet of rushing water can sweep away cars!

Floodwaters wash away buildings, roads, bridges, and people. They often leave behind a layer of **silt** and mud. Each year, floods cost the United States about 6 billion dollars.

Floods are not always catastrophic events. In some places, people look forward to yearly river floods. These floods leave behind nutrient-filled silt that is good for farmland.

THE GREAT FLOOD, 1927

The Great Flood of 1927 was one of the worst natural disasters in U.S. history. After months of heavy rain, the Mississippi River flooded the landscape. More than 23,000 square miles of land were underwater. The flood affected ten states. More than 700,000 people were left homeless.

DEVASTATING DROUGHTS

A drought occurs in areas that receive less rain or snow than normal for a long time. Almost anywhere in the world can suffer from drought.

Water is an important part of life for humans, animals, and plants. But during droughts, water becomes scarce. The ground becomes dusty and cracked. Soil loses nutrients, plants die, and ponds and rivers dry up. Wildfires also become more likely, and farmers may be unable to plant crops.

Humans' overuse of water can make drought conditions worse. To help prevent droughts, people can work to **conserve** water. They can take shorter showers or turn off sprinklers to save water.

DUST BOWL, 1930s

The 1930s Dust Bowl was one of the biggest drought disasters in U.S. history. Severe drought and poor farming practices led to this natural disaster.

The Great Plains had once been grazing land for livestock. Then farmers started farming these prairies. They plowed up the region's native grasses to plant wheat.

The farmland turned to dust when the drought hit. Winds swept away the soil. The native grasses were no longer there to hold the soil in place. The fields could not be farmed. Great clouds of dust darkened the skies for days. Thousands of farming families left their land behind to move west.

A wildfire is an uncontrollable fire that spreads quickly and ferociously. Lightning strikes, campfires, and downed power lines can start wildfires. Something as small as a lit cigarette can spark a massive wildfire.

Wildfires often occur in dry, hot seasons and during droughts. Dry areas are more likely to catch fire. Their thirsty plants are fuel for a wildfire's flames. Strong winds fan the flames, rapidly growing and spreading the fire. As it grows, a wildfire burns everything in its path. Underbrush, trees, and even nearby homes fall victim to the flames and feed the fire.

Firefighters attack wildfires with water. They also set controlled fires to burn up overgrown brush, leaves, shrubs, and trees. This starves wildfires so they can't burn out of control.

Wildfires sometimes threaten people's homes and communities. But wildfires are also a natural and important part of the forest cycle. Wildfires return nutrients to the soil. They burn undergrowth and bring sunlight to the forest floor. Some plants even need wildfires to reproduce. Lodgepole pine trees have cones that only open in fires!

THE BIG BURN, 1910

In a dry August in 1910, a huge wildfire raged in Washington, Montana, and Idaho. An area about the size of Connecticut was devastated by its flames.

An avalanche occurs when large amounts of snow and ice flow down a mountain slope. This snow and ice can speed to 80 miles per hour in seconds. Avalanches slide with deadly force. They wipe out villages and trees in their paths.

An avalanche begins when a slab of snow breaks free from a mountain. The slab starts to slide down the mountain's slope. As it moves, it picks up speed and more snow, ice, and rocks.

A large avalanche may travel at 200 miles per hour. The weight of its snow and ice can reach 1 million tons!

Many avalanches are caused by humans, such as skiers or snowmobilers. Their weight collapses weak layers of snow, sparking the avalanche. Other avalanches are triggered by earthquakes or the weight of fresh snowfall.

? DID YOU KNOW?

A popular myth claims that shouting can set off avalanches. However, voices don't create strong enough vibrations to make the snow start to slide.

PERU, 1970

A magnitude 8.0 earthquake triggered a massive avalanche in Peru in 1970. Snow, ice, and rocks poured down the mountain. They reached speeds of 120 miles per hour. The avalanche completely buried the town of Yungay.

MUDSLIDES:
SLIPPING SLOPES

A mudslide is a disaster in which masses of soft, wet land flow down a slope. These fast-moving disasters can happen with very little warning. A mudslide can travel miles from its source.

Mudslides often happen in areas that have received heavy rainfall. The ground becomes so wet that it can't absorb any more water. This makes the ground soft and unstable. Then the ground gives way and starts to slip.

Like avalanches, mudslides can be extremely destructive. They gain speed and size as they slide downhill. They sweep up boulders, trees, and cars in their paths.

Areas that have experienced wildfires are more likely to have mudslides. Normally, roots of plants and trees hold onto the soil. They make the land more stable. But wildfires burn up the plants and trees. There are no more roots to hold the soil in place.

WASHINGTON STATE, 2014

In 2014, part of a hill collapsed in Washington State, causing a massive mudslide. The area had been hit with vast amounts of rain. The fast-moving, muddy land destroyed 30 homes as it flowed downhill. Some areas were left under 15 feet of mud and debris.

EPIDEMICS AND PANDEMICS:
CONTAGIOUS CATASTROPHES

An epidemic is a widespread outbreak of disease or illness. In an epidemic, an **infectious** disease rapidly sweeps through a community. Thousands of people can become ill in just a short period of time.

During an epidemic, the disease spreads in various ways. Sometimes people infect other people with the disease. This is how influenza and smallpox spread. Other times, animals, such as rats, carry the disease. Still other times, food or water is to blame, as happens with cholera. How people become infected depends on the type of disease.

Eventually an epidemic dies out. This happens when the disease runs out of people to infect. People who have recovered from the disease are **immune** to it. After recovering, their bodies are able to fight it off.

Sometimes an epidemic spreads outside a community. When this happens, the epidemic becomes a pandemic. Pandemics are epidemics that sweep across a wide area, or even the world.

Today, people can easily travel great distances using cars, buses, or airplanes. A person can unknowingly carry a disease from one part of the world to another. This travel can grow an epidemic into a pandemic.

SPANISH FLU, 1918

A massive 1918 pandemic infected people across the globe with the Spanish flu. One-fifth of the world's population became sick. It infected people on almost every continent. Between 20 million and 50 million people died from the Spanish flu.

SOLAR STORMS:
SPACE WEATHER

Earth is not the only place that has weather—space has weather too! Like Earth's weather, space weather creates storms. But space weather doesn't create thunderstorms or hurricanes. Instead, space weather produces very destructive storms called solar storms.

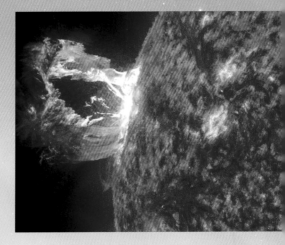

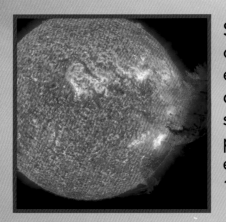

Sometimes explosions happen on the sun's surface. These explosions launch massive clouds of very hot gases into space. These gases are called plasma. The plasma clouds move extremely fast—sometimes up to 1 million miles per hour!

Solar storms happen when the plasma reaches Earth's atmosphere. The plasma clouds blast Earth's **magnetic field** with energy. This sends extra **electric currents** into Earth's atmosphere.

The extra electric currents can disrupt radio signals and GPS systems. They may even interrupt power, leaving people without electricity, water, or telephones.

? DID YOU KNOW?

Near the poles, brilliant, colorful lights dance across the night sky. These are the auroras, or northern lights and southern lights. Auroras become especially intense during solar storms.

CARRINGTON EVENT, 1859

A massive solar storm struck Earth in 1859. The storm's extra currents disrupted the telegraph system. The paper used to record telegraph messages was set on fire!

A solar storm this large has not been seen since. But scientists believe that another solar storm this big could devastate the planet. People could lose power for months. The storm could cause trillions of dollars in damage.

NATURAL DISASTERS QUIZ

1. **Which natural disasters are the most difficult to predict?**

   a) Thunderstorms
   b) Tornadoes
   c) Earthquakes
   d) Hurricanes

2. **Which natural disaster can't be triggered by an earthquake?**

   a) Tornado
   b) Landslide
   c) Tsunami
   d) Volcanic eruption

3. **Which natural disaster is a series of gigantic waves?**

   a) Storm surge
   b) Tsunami
   c) Cyclone
   d) Tidal wave

4. **What is a line of windy thunderstorms called?**

   a) Tsunami
   b) Derecho
   c) Supercell
   d) Cyclone

5. **Where is Tornado Alley located?**

   a) Central United States
   b) Sahara Desert
   c) Northwest United States
   d) Atlantic Ocean

6. **Where do hurricanes form?**

   a) Tropical waters warmer than 80°F
   b) Along the Atlantic coast
   c) Waters colder than 80°F
   d) Cold, icy water in the North Atlantic

7. **Which is the most common weather-related disaster around the world?**

   a) Hurricane
   b) Wildfire
   c) Drought
   d) Flood

8. **What type of natural disaster was the 1930s Dust Bowl?**

   a) Tornado
   b) Drought
   c) Flood
   d) Derecho

Answers: 1) c 2) a 3) b 4) b 5) a 6) a 7) d 8) b

GLOSSARY

Active volcanoes volcanoes that have erupted in the past 10,000 years

Atmosphere the mass of gases surrounding a planet or moon

Conserve to protect or save

Electric currents the flows of electricity

Evaporates absorbs water into the air

Immune unable to become infected

Infectious able to be passed to people from the environment, animals, or other people

Magnetic field the area around a magnetic object

Mantle the layer of Earth between the crust and the core

Silt material similar to sand or clay that is carried by water

Tectonic plate a massive, irregularly shaped slab of rock that divides the Earth's crust and on which the continents move

SOLAR STORM

TSUNAMI

EARTHQUAKE

AVALANCHE

HURRICANE

TORNADO

A tsunami is a series of massive, mighty waves, called a wave train. Underwater earthquakes, volcano eruptions, and landslides may launch tsunamis. As they reach land, tsunami waves may grow into 100-foot-tall walls of water.

Explosions on the Sun's surface can create solar storms. These storms send electrical currents into Earth's atmosphere. The currents disrupt GPS systems, interrupt power, and harm satellites. They can also create intense, colorful auroras in the night sky.

Avalanches occur when massive slabs of snow break free from mountains. As the slabs slide down, they gain speed, pick up boulders, and sweep away trees.

An earthquake occurs when tectonic plates bump into each other. This causes the ground to shake violently. More than 50,000 earthquakes happen each year.

A tornado is a windstorm that has a spinning, funnel-shaped cloud. It forms out of violent thunderstorms. Tornadoes have the fastest winds on Earth, and they can spin at up to 300 miles per hour!

Hurricanes are swirling tropical storms that form over the ocean. When they strike land, they bring heavy rains and powerful winds. They die out when they blow over land or cold waters.

WORLD WONDERS

Kaitlyn DiPerna

CONTENTS

WONDER-FILLED WORLD

Wonder is the feeling that you get when you see something unexpectedly beautiful, especially for the first time. There are many places in our world that can leave you in awe and admiration. Some of these places are natural wonders like massive mountains, broad rivers, or underwater **ecosystems**. Some of these places are manmade and we marvel at their beauty, size, and history.

Underwater Ecosystem: Great Barrier Reef

Massive Migration: The Serengeti

Impressive Tombs: The Pyramids

Ancient Mystery: Easter Island Statues

Our world is home to countless wonders. There are many ways of listing world wonders. This book is a short list of some of the world's most impressive wonders. You can make your own list of wonders, and check them off as you visit them, one by one.

THE GRAND CANYON:
MILLIONS OF YEARS IN THE MAKING

A trickle of water may not look like much, but a large amount of fast-moving water can change the landscape into something to marvel at. It took millions of years for the Colorado River to carve the massive Grand Canyon in Arizona. The powerful river carved a **canyon** that is over 270 miles long, up to 18 miles wide, and a mile deep.

Arizona

Horseshoe Bend

When you look at the walls of the canyon, it is like you are looking back in time. The rocks of the Grand Canyon are some of the oldest on Earth. The red, brown, and gold stripes in the walls of the Grand Canyon each show a different time in Earth's **geologic** history.

The Grand Canyon is home to endangered California condors and bighorn sheep as well as rattlesnakes and coyotes.

President Theodore Roosevelt was known as a protector of America's wilderness. During his presidency, he named the Grand Canyon a National Monument. In 1919, the Grand Canyon became a National Park.

Millions of visitors come to the Grand Canyon each year. Some visit to hike the miles of trails, others raft down the Colorado River. Some visit to watch the colors of the canyon in the light of spectacular sunrises and sunsets. The bravest visitors stand on the Grand Canyon Skywalk just outside of the park. The horseshoe-shaped skywalk has a glass floor and is suspended over 4,000 feet above the canyon floor—that's higher than the world's tallest skyscraper!

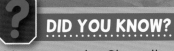 **DID YOU KNOW?**

Visitors to the Skywalk are given shoe covers to protect them from slipping and prevent them from scratching the glass floor!

TOP OF THE WORLD: MOUNT EVEREST

Most commercial airplanes fly at an **altitude** of around 30,000 feet. The next time you see a plane high in the sky, imagine a mountain peak where the plane is—that is the height of Mount Everest! At over 29,000 feet, Mount Everest is the tallest mountain above sea level in the world.

Mount Everest is almost 60 million years old, but it wasn't declared the tallest mountain in the world until 1852. Buried deep in the Himalaya Mountain Range on the border of Nepal and China, the mountain is named after George Everest, a British **surveyor** who helped to locate and measure many of the Himalaya Mountains.

? DID YOU KNOW?

Movement of the plates beneath Mount Everest cause it to rise about one eighth of an inch each year and move northeast each year at about the same rate.

In 1953, two climbers stood on the highest summit on Earth for the first time: Sir Edmund Hillary, from New Zealand, and Tenzing Norgay, from Nepal.

Since then, over 4,000 people have made it to the top of Mount Everest. However, climbing the mountain is no small feat. High winds, sheer cliffs of ice, deep **crevasses**, and summit temperatures that never go above freezing, make Everest incredibly dangerous. Climbers are also challenged by the lack of oxygen. As the altitude above sea level increases, there is less oxygen in the air. To help them breathe, most climbers carry oxygen tanks.

GREAT GEYSERS
OF YELLOWSTONE NATIONAL PARK

The first national park in the world is unlike anywhere else on the planet. Geysers blast boiling hot water hundreds of feet into the air. Hot springs are ringed in rainbow colors. Mud pots belch steam. And nearly three hundred waterfalls tumble to the ground. Yellowstone National Park is filled with amazing **geothermal** features heated to boiling by a layer of hot molten rock beneath the ground.

Wyoming

Nearly all of Yellowstone National Park is within the borders of Wyoming. Yellowstone National Park is a little larger than two Rhode Islands, but is home to 10,000 thermal features and half of the planet's geysers. The hot springs of Yellowstone National Park are actually the hottest springs in the world. The water can reach temperatures around 189°F!

 DID YOU KNOW?

The geyser "Old Faithful" received its name because of its regular eruptions. Old Faithful erupts every 35 to 120 minutes for 1.5 to 5 minutes. Its maximum height ranges from 90 to 184 feet.

Yellowstone National Park is on top of an underground volcano that is so powerful it is called a "supervolcano." This supervolcano is very active: Yellowstone experiences between one and 1,600 earthquakes every year! Most of the park is covered in rocks and lava flows from volcanic eruptions.

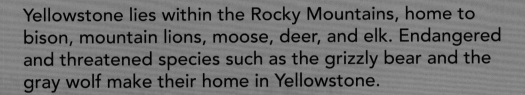

Yellowstone lies within the Rocky Mountains, home to bison, mountain lions, moose, deer, and elk. Endangered and threatened species such as the grizzly bear and the gray wolf make their home in Yellowstone.

 **DID YOU KNOW?**

The vivid colors of the hot springs come from a form of bacteria.

Grand Prismatic Spring

THE GREAT BARRIER REEF:
UNDERWATER WORLD

The Great Barrier Reef is alive! In fact, it is the largest living structure in the world. The Great Barrier Reef is so large that it can be seen from space!

The Great Barrier Reef is made up of 3,000 separate coral reefs. A coral reef doesn't form quickly. First, tiny coral polyps attach themselves together. Then the polyps create a hard stony skeleton, forming a reef. The Great Barrier Reef has been an underwater building project for more than 20 million years!

The Great Barrier Reef is located in the Coral Sea, off the northeastern coast of Australia. Measuring about 135,000 square miles, it's about half the size of Texas. But it is growing, very slowly, less than one inch each year.

Coral reefs cover less than one percent of the ocean floor, but the warm shallow waters of the Great Barrier Reef are home to twenty-five percent of all marine life on the planet.

Over 400 different types of coral make up the reef, which is also home to colorful anemones, sponges, clams, and worms. Sea turtles, sharks, seahorses, stingrays, and over 1,500 different species of fish all depend on the reef for food, shelter, and survival.

clownfish

angelfish

reef shark

sea turtle

This giant living organism is very delicate. Fishing, pollution, and climate change can all damage the fragile reef. A thirty-year study found that the Great Barrier Reef has lost nearly half its coral, mainly due to storm damage and the overpopulation of crown of thorns starfish, which eat the coral. It is incredibly important to protect this amazing underwater world and its inhabitants.

WALKING THE GREAT WALL OF CHINA

The Great Wall of China is not actually one long wall. It is a system of many walls that stretch thousands of miles across the northern borders of China. There are a few sections that have trenches instead of a wall or the natural landscape (a mountain or river) is used in place of a wall.

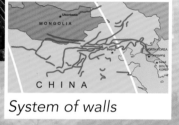

System of walls

Nearly 2,750 years ago, China was divided into different kingdoms that were at war with each other. The kingdoms built walls from wood and stones around their territory for protection.

Around 500 years later, one kingdom, the Qin, defeated their rivals and China became one empire. The Qin emperor needed to protect the new territory, so he ordered construction of an even longer wall along China's northern border. This wall would be made of bricks, and have watch towers for troops to stand guard against enemies from the north. Guards along the tower could signal each other using smoke, fires, or lanterns.

It took more than 250 years and close to 2 million workers to build the main part of the Great Wall. The work was difficult and dangerous. Hundreds of thousands of laborers died during construction. Many workers were buried within the walls—their skeletons are still there today!

Genghis Kahn

But over thousands of years, the wall couldn't keep out China's enemies. Genghis Kahn, the leader of Mongolia, broke through the wall in 1211 and conquered China. After nearly 150 years, the Chinese pushed their northern enemies back out of China and rebuilt the wall to be even stronger and longer.

The wall was built, torn down, built again, and added to over thousands of years. More recently, sections of the walls have been torn down or collapsed. The Great Wall of China is the longest manmade structure ever built, estimated to be over 13,100 miles long. But even today, the exact length of the Great Wall is still unknown.

THE MASSIVE MIGRATION
OF THE SERENGETI

Serengeti National Park is just a bit larger than Connecticut, but it is home to the most varied collection of land animals on the planet. Over seventy species of mammals and 500 species of birds can be found on the Serengeti.

Most of the Serengeti is savanna—wide, flat grasslands with few trees. The name "Serengeti" means "endless plains" in the language of the Maasai people who live around the plains.

The climate of the Serengeti is usually hot and dry. But two rainy seasons, March–May and October–November, bring heavy rains. The animals depend on the rains to grow the grass that they eat. The rains flood the plain and create rivers and shallow ponds that the animals use for watering holes.

The National Park in Tanzania is famous for its amazing animal migration. Over 1 million wildebeest, about 200,000 zebras, and 300,000 Thomson's gazelle head north in April, May, and June, and then return south for the rains in October and November.

The Serengeti is home to lions, leopards, rhinoceroses, buffalo, and African elephants. These animals are sometimes called "the big five." The big five were once the animals that hunters wanted to capture. Today, they are the animals that people on safari would most like to see.

French engineer Gustave Eiffel designed and built the Eiffel Tower. It was meant to serve as the entrance arch to the 1889 World's Fair in Paris. The plan was for the tower to be taken apart after twenty years.

When the tower was built beside the River Seine, it was the tallest structure in the world, about the height of an eighty-story building. It takes 2,731 steps to reach the top of the tower. The Eiffel Tower held the title of tallest building in the world for forty-one years. Today, it still holds the title of the tallest building in Paris.

1,063 feet

The iron tower took two years, two months, and five days to build. To prevent the iron from rusting, the Eiffel Tower must be completely repainted every seven years.

When the tower was first built, many people thought it was ugly. A famous French writer climbed the tower each day, explaining that it was the only place in the city from which he couldn't see the hideous tower. But over time, the tower was accepted.

Today, the Eiffel Tower is one of the most visited monuments in the world. There are three levels for visitors: the first and second levels have restaurants, and the third level has a platform with incredible views of the city.

Though the Eiffel Tower wasn't meant to be a permanent structure, it has been reinforced to stand forever as a symbol of the city of Paris and the nation of France.

? DID YOU KNOW?

The warmth from the sun heats up the iron, making it expand. The tower can expand to be up to seven inches taller as well as lean up to seven inches!

ANCIENT TOMBS:
THE PYRAMIDS OF GIZA

About five thousand years ago, pharaohs ruled the powerful ancient Egyptian **civilization**. The pharaohs were kings and queens, but they were also seen as gods and goddesses. When pharaohs died, their mummified bodies were placed in enormous burial tombs: the pyramids.

Pyramid of Menkaure

Pyramid of Khafre

Pyramid of Khufu (the Great Pyramid)

The Pyramids of Giza are just outside Egypt's capital of Cairo, but they are surrounded by desert. In Giza, there are three main pyramids plus the Great Sphinx.

The Pyramids of Giza have stood for nearly 5,000 years. It is estimated that it took twenty-three years and up to 25,000 workers to build the Great Pyramid. The pyramids were built by an enormous workforce including haulers, masons, mortar-mixers, and even cooks and clothes-makers.

The base of the Great Pyramid is almost a perfect square. The blocks were held together with a mortar that is even harder than the stones. Even today, scientists have not been able to figure out what the mortar was made of.

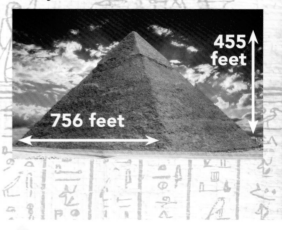

455 feet

756 feet

The Great Sphinx was part of the monument for the Pharaoh Khafre. The face was carved to look like Khafre, but the body is that of a lion. The Sphinx is 240 feet long and 66 feet high.

The original entrance of the Great Pyramid is more than fifty feet off the ground. Inside, dark, narrow hallways lead to two burial chambers, one for the king, and another for the queen. Pharaohs were buried with treasures for them to bring to the afterlife. But in the thousands of years since they were buried, many robbers have stolen the jewels, artifacts, and even the mummified pharaohs. Today, many museums have Egyptian artifacts and mummies on display for visitors to marvel at.

THE NORTHERN LIGHTS:
SPIRITS IN THE SKY

Colorful curtains dance across the sky. Glimmering clouds hover. Ribbons of light sparkle above the Earth. Seeing the Northern Lights is a magical experience.

The light displays are called auroras and can only be seen above Earth's magnetic North and South Poles. The Northern Lights are called the Aurora Borealis. Aurora was the Roman goddess of the dawn and "boreas" is the Greek word for north wind.

People native to the area around the North Pole had many stories to explain the lights. Some thought the lights were powerful dancing spirits. Others thought they were spirits of animals. Some were afraid of the lights, thinking they were a sign of bad things to come.

These mysterious lights in the night sky occur about fifty miles above the Earth's surface. The auroras are caused by particles in Earth's atmosphere bumping against particles released from the Sun's atmosphere. Depending on what types of particles are colliding and how high they are in the atmosphere, different colors are produced. Higher in the atmosphere, red lights appear. Closer to the Earth, green, blue, or pale purple lights can be seen.

The best places to see the Northern Lights are in northwest Canada and Alaska, and the southern tip of Greenland and Iceland. They are most common during the coldest months: September through early March. But weeks may go by without any activity. Some of these light displays can last for hours, others for only a few minutes. And it is never the same show twice.

DID YOU KNOW?

Earth is not the only planet to experience auroras. Auroras have been observed on every planet except Mercury. Even Jupiter's three major moons have auroras!

THE MYSTERIOUS
MOAI OF EASTER ISLAND

Easter Island

Way out in the middle of the South Pacific Ocean, lies a lonely little island named Easter Island. Over 1,000 years ago, people from the Polynesian Islands rowed canoes thousands of miles across the ocean and landed on this tiny island. These settlers called their new home Rapa Nui.

At its height, the Rapa Nui population numbered around 15,000 people. But disease, overpopulation, and deforestation devastated the island and its people. In 1877, there were only 111 Rapa Nui people left.

There is no written history of the Rapa Nui people, so much of their story is a mystery. Easter Island's most famous mystery is the nearly 900 giant stone statues that can be found all over the island. The thousand-year-old statues are known as "moai." Many people believe the moai were meant to honor the dead, but no one knows for sure.

Some 400 statues in various stages of completion can be found at the **quarry**, where the volcanic stones for the moai were gathered. A few hundred are standing on platforms. The rest are scattered around the island, where they were abandoned, probably on their way to the place where they would be raised onto platforms.

Part of what makes these statues so impressive is their size. Most were around thirteen feet tall and weighed around fourteen tons, more than two elephants. The largest moai isn't standing, but if it were, it would be over thirty feet tall. The other unsolved mystery of the moai is how the Rapa Nui people moved these massive statues.

Over time, wind and rain have worn the sculptures away, and many have toppled over. But the mystery of the meaning of the massive moai remains.

127

Amazon Rainforest

The Amazon is the planet's largest rain forest. The rainforest spans over 2 million square miles into nine countries, and covers almost half of Brazil. Lots of rivers, rainfall, and warm temperatures create a lush **habitat** full of jungle trees, plants, and animals.

The Amazon Rainforest is home to more wildlife than anywhere else on Earth. Several million species of animals, insects, birds and plants live in the Amazon. It's estimated that the rainforest holds thousands more species that haven't yet been discovered.

? **DID YOU KNOW?**

One in ten of the world's known species can be found in the Amazon Rainforest.

The Amazon River, which flows through the rainforest, carries more water than any other river on the planet. If the next seven largest rivers on Earth were combined, they still wouldn't hold as much water as the Amazon!

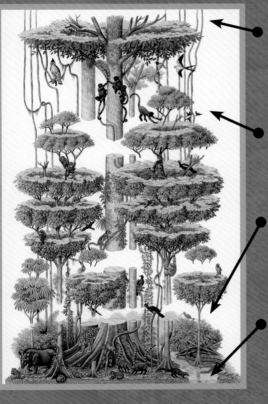

The rainforest is divided into four layers:

Emergent Layer: A small number of very tall trees reach through the canopy into this layer where only a few birds, bats, and butterflies may perch.

Canopy Layer: The treetops and high branches of the canopy layer are home to many animals, as there is plenty of food here.

Understory Layer: Leopards, snakes, and lizards all live in the understory among the short trees and shrubs of the Amazon.

Forest Floor: In this level, everything decays quickly since there is very little sunlight reaching the forest floor.

Large areas of the Amazon Rainforest are being cut down to make room for farming or grazing land for cattle. Almost twenty percent of the Amazon Rainforest has been lost in the last forty years. Countries are now taking steps to save the rainforest and all its inhabitants, discovered and undiscovered.

LABOR OF LOVE:
THE TAJ MAHAL

It is said that Mumtaz Mahal was one of the most beautiful Persian princesses. In her honor, Emperor Shah Jahan built one of the world's most beautiful tombs.

The Taj Mahal is an above-ground burial chamber in northern India. Emperor Shah Jahan built the elaborate tomb over 350 years ago for his third wife, Mumtaz Mahal, who died while giving birth to her fourteenth child.

Inside the beautiful building, Shah Jahan and Mumtaz Mahal lie side by side in plain graves.

Known as one of the most picturesque buildings in the world, the Taj Mahal took twenty-two years and 22,000 workers to build. The Taj Mahal is made of white marble from around the world that was carted to India by 1,000 elephants! The marble is carved and painted with different designs and calligraphy. There were once precious stones set into the walls, but British troops stole many of the stones in the 1800s.

The **symmetrical** tomb has an arch-shaped doorway and a dome that measures 115 feet tall. The gardens surrounding the Taj Mahal contain pathways, pools, fountains, flowers, and fruit trees.

The white marble of the Taj Mahal seems to change color in the rising and setting sun, making the experience of visiting the tomb a magical experience.

GLADIATORS' STAGE: COLOSSEUM

Even though the Colosseum may be called a "ruin," it is still spectacular. This giant concrete and stone structure has held the title of largest outdoor arena in the world since it was first built nearly 2,000 years ago.

Roman Empire

The Colosseum is a symbol of the glory of the Roman Empire. The Romans ruled over much of Europe and Northern Africa for 500 years. They were known for their excellence in engineering and architecture, skills that can still be seen in the construction of the Colosseum.

It is estimated that 50,000 people could fit inside the Colosseum to watch the spectacular shows. Pretend battles were put on for entertainment. Real battles between gladiators and wild animals were watched for sport. Elephants, rhinoceroses, lions, bears, and crocodiles were brought to the arena from all over the world to fight gladiators.

For some shows, the arena floor was flooded with water. Later, trap doors were added that led to hallways, chambers, and cages beneath. Animals and gladiators could be raised up to the floor through the trap doors.

? DID YOU KNOW?

The completion of the Colosseum was marked by a hundred-day celebration of battles. In those hundred days over 10,000 wild animals were killed for the crowds.

When the Roman Empire collapsed almost 1,500 years ago, the Colosseum was abandoned. Parts of it were taken for use in other new buildings. But what's left is a remarkable ruin.

WORLD WONDERS QUIZ

1. **Which river flows through the Grand Canyon?**

   a) The Colorado
   b) The Arizona
   c) The Mississippi
   d) The Grand Canyon River

2. **How tall is Mount Everest?**

   a) 39,000 feet above sea level
   b) 9,000 feet above sea level
   c) 29,000 feet above sea level
   d) 30,000 feet above sea level

3. **Which CANNOT be found while visiting Yellowstone National Park?**

   a) Old Faithful
   b) Grand Canyon
   c) Grand Prismatic Spring
   d) Endangered gray wolves

4. **Which animal CANNOT be found in Serengeti National Park?**

   a) Bison
   b) Wildebeest
   c) Leopards
   d) Rhinoceros

5. The Eiffel Tower was built for which event?

a) The 1889 Summer Olympics
b) The 1889 French Open
c) The 1889 World Olympics
d) The 1889 World's Fair

6. What are the massive stone statues on Easter Island called?

a) Moai
b) Maori
c) Rapa Nui
d) Easter Island Statues

7. In the name "Aurora Borealis," what does "boreas" mean?

a) dawn
b) northern lights
c) north wind
d) aurora

8. Whose graves can be found inside the Taj Mahal?

a. Mumtaz Mahal
b. Mumtaz Mahal and Shah Jahan
c. Taj Mahal
d. Taj Mahal and Shah Jahan

Answers: 1) a 2) c 3) b 4) a 5) d 6) a 7) c 8) b

GLOSSARY

Altitude the height of something above sea level

Canyon a deep valley with steep rock sides, often with a river or stream flowing through it

Civilization the way of life of a people

Crevasses deep openings in land or ice caused by a split or crack

Dormant not active

Ecosystems a community of living things and their environment

Geologic science of Earth's history as recorded in rocks

Geothermal heat from the Earth's interior

Habitat place where a plant or animal naturally lives

Quarry place for digging stones to use in building

Surveyor a person who maps the land

Symmetrical both sides the same

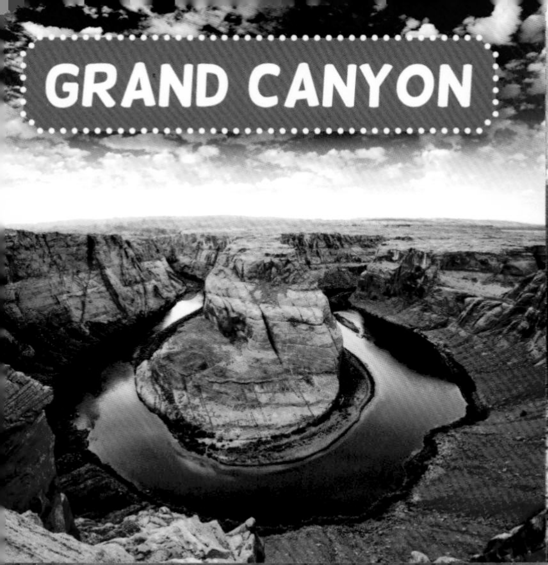

GRAND CANYON

GREAT BARRIER REEF

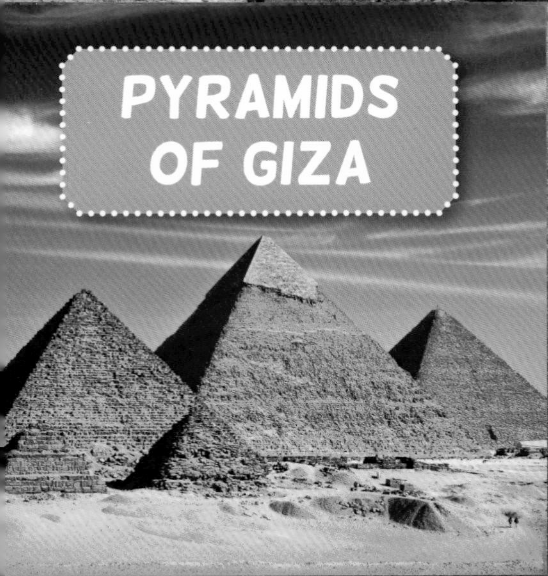

PYRAMIDS OF GIZA

AMAZON RAINFOREST

EIFFEL TOWER

MOUNT EVEREST

Location: Coral Sea, northeast of Australia
Size: 135,000 square miles

The Great Barrier Reef is home to around 940 islands and cays, close to 3,000 coral reefs, 411 types of coral, and 1,600 species of fish.

Location: Arizona, United States
Size: 1,904 square miles

The Colorado River carved nearly a mile into the rock to form the canyon.

Location: South America
Size: 2,300,000 square miles

The Amazon Rainforest is home to more wildlife than anywhere else on Earth.

Location: Egypt
Height: 480 feet (Great Pyramid)

The pyramids were giant royal tombs for kings and queens of ancient Egypt.

Location: China and Nepal border
Height: 29,029 feet

The first men to reach Mount Everest's summit were Sir Edmund Hillary and Tenzing Norgay, in 1953.

Location: Paris, France
Height: 986 feet

The Eiffel Tower was only meant to be temporary, but has been reinforced to stand for years to come.

OCEAN
HABITATS

Emily Rose Oachs

CONTENTS

WHAT IS THE OCEAN?

Arctic

Atlantic

Pacific

Pacific

Indian

Southern

The ocean is very important to life on Earth. The ocean holds 97 percent of Earth's water and covers two-thirds of the Earth's surface. The water that covers most of Earth is divided into five oceans: the Pacific, Atlantic, Indian, Arctic, and Southern (also known as the Antarctic) Oceans.

The ocean is one continuous string of habitats, each flowing into the next. A habitat is a home for plants and animals. Some ocean animals may live in just one habitat for their entire lives. Other animals may travel freely between the different habitats.

The oceans hold the richest variety of life on Earth. Whether the ocean is cold and icy or warm and tropical, many different kinds of animals call the ocean home.

TIDE POOLS:
POCKETS OF SEA LIFE

As the **tide** rises along the seashore, shallow holes in coastal rocks are filled with water. Many creatures live in and around these pockets of seawater. These small pools are known as tide pools.

Twice a day the sea level rises and falls along the seashore. This is known as the tides. The tides are caused by the moon's gravity. As the moon revolves around the Earth, its gravity pulls the water on Earth toward it. When the moon pulls water toward shore, it is high tide. Tide pools are underwater at high tide. When it draws the water away from shore, it is low tide. Tide pools are revealed at low tide.

Sea stars are at home in rocky tide pools. Each of a sea star's arms has hundreds of tube feet to help it crawl and stick to hard surfaces. Many sea stars have five arms, but some have more than forty! Sea stars can be as small as a human hand or more than three feet across.

Sometimes a **predator** breaks off a sea star's arm. The sea star can grow a new arm in its place!

Sea urchins look like living pincushions. Moveable spines and tentacle-like tube feet grow from their round bodies. Their spines may be poisonous, and some grow to be eight inches long!

 DID YOU KNOW?

Sea stars and sea urchins do not have eyes or brains. Water pumps through their bodies instead of blood.

141

Most crabs grow their own shells to protect their soft bodies—but not hermit crabs! Hermit crabs live in the empty shells of other animals, such as snails. As hermit crabs grow, they must trade their old, small shells for larger shells.

Turban snails grow spiraled shells for protection. Like other snails, a turban snail uses a flat, muscular "foot" to move. If threatened, the snail pulls itself into its shell. Then it blocks the shell's opening with its foot.

Blue-ringed octopuses are small eight-armed creatures. They carry enough poison to kill twenty-six humans. When disturbed, bright blue rings appear on their tan skin. These blue rings mean one thing: Look out!

Oystercatchers wade along the ocean's shore on their pink legs. They search for food left on shore as the tide goes out. Oystercatchers have flat, orange bills. These bills easily pry open the shells of mussels, oysters, and clams.

A massive, flexible pouch of skin hangs from a pelican's bill. This pouch can hold three gallons of water!

Pelicans use the pouch to catch fish. They dive into the ocean to scoop up a meal. Then the pelicans drain out the water and swallow the fish whole!

ROCKY SHORES:
OCEAN COASTS

The rocky shore is a habitat for animals that live among rocks on the coast. Because of the tides, these animals live where the **sea level** is constantly changing. Sometimes the animals are pounded by the

waves. Other times they are exposed to the sun and have very little water. These animals are able to live in many different conditions.

Octopuses live throughout the ocean. Some, like the red octopus, hide between underwater rocks along the shore. They have soft, boneless bodies and eight arms lined with suckers.

Because they are soft and flexible, even large octopuses can squeeze into tight nooks. A fifty-pound octopus can fit through a two-inch hole!

? **DID YOU KNOW?**

Octopuses have three hearts that pump blue blood through their bodies!

Seals and sea lions often leave the ocean to lay on the rocks of the rocky shores.

To move on land, sea lions shift their back flippers under their bodies to walk on all fours. Seals use their stomach muscles to wriggle like a caterpillar.

Sea lions and seals can be difficult to tell apart. Sea lions have small flaps over their ears, but seals only have ear holes. Also, seals spend more time in the water than sea lions. Some seals only come to shore once a year.

sea lion

seal

CORAL REEFS:
LIVING STRUCTURES

Hidden beneath the warm ocean's surface are huge, colorful living structures—coral reefs. Coral reefs cover less than 1 percent of the Earth's surface. But 25 percent of the planet's ocean **species** call coral reefs home!

Corals are brightly colored, soft-bodied polyps. One end is hard and solid, and the other end has a mouth and stinging **tentacles**. Some corals are hard and rigid, but others are soft and flexible. They can look like brains, lettuce, or feathers!

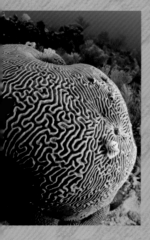

Corals live in groups, or colonies. A coral attaches to a hard surface, and then it multiplies and connects with other corals to form a colony.

Corals leave behind their hard skeletons when they die. These slowly build up into a coral reef. Most of the coral reefs we see today are between 5,000 and 10,000 years old.

Nudibranchs are known for their bizarre shapes and bright colors. Nudibranchs are soft-bodied sea slugs. They can range from ¼ inch to 12 inches long. Some nudibranchs are poisonous, and their bright bodies warn predators to stay away!

Giant clams can grow to be four feet across and weigh over 500 pounds. Once they attach themselves to a spot on the reef, the giant mollusks will stay there for the rest of their lives.

Pufferfish have a unique defense. If a predator threatens them, they gulp lots of water to inflate like a ball. When they puff up, dangerous spines stand out from their bodies. These scare attackers away.

Pufferfish are also poisonous. A single pufferfish holds enough poison to kill thirty humans! If a predator eats a pufferfish, the fish's poison may kill the predator.

Before they sleep, parrot fish wrap themselves in a layer of mucus. The mucus masks their scent. This protects them from being found by predators as they sleep.

Bright blues and electric yellows cover the body of a queen angelfish. The bright colors help the queen angelfish to blend in with the coral reef.

Sea horses are small fish with small fins. They curl their tails around coral and plants so they won't drift away. Sometimes sea horses travel through the ocean by clinging to pieces of drifting seaweed.

Pygmy sea horses are some of the smallest sea horses. They only grow to be less than one inch long. A pygmy sea horse's color and texture almost perfectly match those of a sea fan. This tiny animal is nearly invisible in the coral!

Clown fish and sea anemones live together in the coral reef.

Sea anemones are colorful creatures related to corals and jellyfish. Like corals, sea anemones are soft, tube-shaped polyps. One end of a sea anemone's body attaches to a rock. The other end has a mouth surrounded by tentacles.

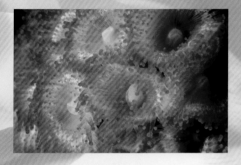

Sea anemones wait for their prey to swim close. Then they sting their prey with poisonous tentacles.

Clownfish are bright orange fish with white stripes. These fish are covered in a mucus that protects them from a sea anemone's sting. Clownfish are safe from predators when they're in sea anemones.

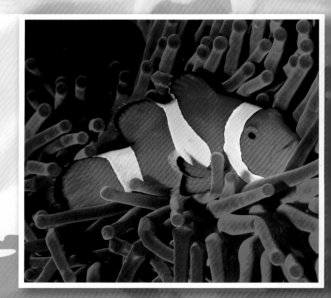

A lionfish's showy fins look beautiful as it swims through the coral reef. But these needle-like fins deliver a powerful sting. To scare predators, a lionfish spreads its fins, and its long poisonous spines stand on end.

Bluestripe snappers school near coral reefs to protect themselves. Schooling is when many fish swim together in a tight pack. When fish do this, predators may mistake the school for one large fish. Or it can be difficult for the predators to pick out a single fish to attack. This means that a fish is more likely to survive when it is surrounded by many other fish.

KELP FOREST:
UNDERWATER JUNGLE

A kelp forest is an underwater jungle made up of many stalks of kelp, or large floating algae. These plants grow in shallow waters where there is a lot of sunlight. They can stretch over 100 feet from the ocean floor to the surface. They sometimes grow 18 inches in a single day!

Some animals use the kelp to hide from predators. Other animals find food in this underwater forest, eating other fish or even the kelp itself.

Leafy sea dragons rely on **camouflage** for protection in kelp forests. These fish have frilly bodies, leaflike fins, and brown and yellow skin. They gently sway with the plants in the water. They look like pieces of floating seaweed or kelp!

Sea otters are smart mammals that use tools like humans do. They use rocks like hammers to open the shells of mussels or clams. A sea otter stores its rocks in an underarm pouch to use later.

When they aren't swimming in the kelp forest, sea otters like to float on top of it. They wrap themselves in kelp when they sleep. This keeps them from drifting away. Some sea otters hold hands to stay together. Mother sea otters float on their backs and balance their pups on their bellies.

ICY WATERS:
THE ARCTIC AND ANTARCTIC

The Arctic and Antarctic Oceans are located at the most northern and southern points on Earth. Life in the extreme cold of the North and South Poles is not easy. The species that live here must adapt to the icy waters.

Antarctic Animals

Emperor penguins gather on the Antarctic ice. These flightless seabirds form large groups, or colonies. They huddle together on the frozen landscape to keep warm.

A female emperor penguin lays her egg, and then she dives into the ocean to hunt for food. The male penguin is left to care for the egg. He balances it on top of his feet and covers it with a flap of warm skin. He doesn't eat at all until the female returns two months later!

Arctic Animals

Walruses are massive mammals that live far in the north. Large tusks grow from their whiskery mouths. These tusks can grow to be three feet long. Walruses can use these tusks to haul themselves out of the water.

A walrus's lumbering body may weigh over 3,000 pounds. Like many other ocean mammals, walruses have blubber under their thick skin. Blubber is a layer of fat on their bodies. It keeps them warm in the Arctic's chilly temperatures.

A long swordlike tooth, or tusk, grows from male narwhals' upper lips. These spiraled tusks may grow to ten feet long! In the Arctic, narwhals' tusks poke through the water's surface as these mammals swim in the icy waters.

Out in the open ocean, there are no coral reefs to hide in or kelp forests to swim through. Animals must find other ways to protect themselves. Some creatures use camouflage, while others have stinging tentacles. Still others swim so fast that they break the ocean surface and "fly" through the air.

Sea turtles have hard shells and paddle-like flippers. Many sea turtles lay their eggs far away from their feeding grounds. They may **migrate** thousands of miles to lay their eggs. Sea turtles rely on Earth's warm **currents** to travel through the open ocean. They use the currents like highways to migrate!

 **DID YOU KNOW?**

Leatherback sea turtles travel up to 1,400 miles to lay their eggs!

Puffins build their nests on steep cliffs along the seashore. These seabirds spend most of the year out at sea. In the ocean, puffins flap their wings underwater to swim and dive for fish. They float on the waves when they need a break from flying or swimming.

Jellyfish live throughout the ocean, whether the waters are cold or warm or deep or shallow. They are 97 percent water, and they don't have brains, hearts, or bones. These see-through, bell-shaped creatures have stinging tentacles.

? DID YOU KNOW?

A group of jellyfish is called a smack!

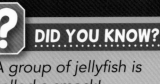

Whales and dolphins may look like fish, but they're really mammals. Because they are mammals, they must come to the surface to breathe. Dolphins and whales breathe using special nostrils called blowholes located on top of their heads.

Dolphins are small toothed whales. They communicate with other dolphins using whistles, clicks, chirps, and by slapping their tails. These noises say the dolphins are happy, sad, scared, or want to play.

Orcas are commonly called "killer whales," but they are actually the largest members of the dolphin family. They are fierce predators. They use their 4-inch-long teeth to tear up their **prey**. Sometimes they steal seals right off of the ice!

Gray whales are long-distance swimmers. Each year, gray whales travel over 12,000 miles round trip as they migrate from the Arctic to warmer waters near the equator.

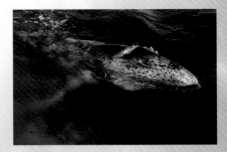

Blue whales weigh around 150 tons and can grow to nearly 100 feet long! They are the biggest creatures on the planet. But they feed on some of the ocean's smallest—krill. Krill are little shrimp-like creatures. A blue whale eats four tons of krill in a single day!

krill

? DID YOU KNOW?

Most whale species swallow their food whole without chewing it. They have fringed plates on their gums that act like a strainer. These plates, called baleen, trap the krill, but allow water to flow back out of the whale's mouth.

Some of the world's most ferocious fish live in the open ocean: sharks. More than 400 species of sharks live in the ocean.

Sharks are often feared because of their many sharp teeth. If a shark loses a tooth, it will replace the tooth. In fact, they have rows of teeth waiting in line.

Sharks may be some of the ocean's most ferocious predators, but remoras have nothing to fear from many of them. A remora gets free rides through the water from sharks. It uses a sucker on its head to attach to the shark. The remora then keeps the shark clean by eating parasites from its body.

Tiger sharks are vicious fish. Their jagged teeth and strong jaws can rip through sea turtle shells!

Hammerhead sharks have long, wide heads. They have one eye and one nostril at each end of their heads. Most sharks are solitary creatures, but hammerheads swim through the ocean in schools.

Manta rays are fish with flat, triangular bodies. They are closely related to sharks. To move, manta rays flap their wing-like fins. These fish are so powerful that they can leap out of the water!

Fish are cold-blooded animals that can be found in both fresh and salt water. They have gills that bring oxygen into their bodies. Fish are usually covered in scales. They also have fins instead of arms and legs. From warm, shallow water to the deepest, darkest depths, fish live in every part of the ocean.

Herring are common prey for tuna, salmon, orcas, and finback whales. These silver fish travel through the open ocean in massive schools. Millions may swim together in a single school!

A sailfish has a tall, sail-like fin and a long, spear-like nose. This strange fish is the speediest in the ocean. It can launch itself out of the water at 68 miles per hour!

Sharp, strong teeth line the snout of a largetooth sawfish. Its long saw-like nose is called a rostrum. The sawfish uses its rostrum like a sword, attacking prey with powerful swipes.

Molas have enormous, flat bodies that can weigh 5,000 pounds! Molas often swim near the surface of the open ocean. Their silver dorsal fins poke above the surface. These tall fins have been mistaken for shark fins!

DEEP SEA:
INTO THE DEPTHS

Miles below the open ocean's surface is the floor of the ocean. This is the deep sea—the deepest, darkest part of the ocean. Here the water is nearly freezing. No sunlight reaches the deep ocean floor. This deep, dark, cold environment is home to some of the strangest creatures on the planet.

? DID YOU KNOW?

The Mariana Trench is the deepest point in the ocean and on Earth itself. It plunges 36,198 feet below the water's surface. The Mariana Trench is deeper than Mount Everest is tall.

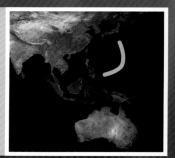

There is no sunlight in the deep sea, but the waters still spark and shine in the dark. Some animals in the deep sea make their own light! This is called **bioluminescence**. Animals use bioluminescence to attract a mate, find prey, or hide from predators.

Anglerfish fish live deep in the Atlantic and Antarctic Oceans. The female anglerfish has a spine attached to the top of her head. This spine is like a fishing pole. Its tip lights up to attract prey.

Male anglerfish look very different from females. Males are much smaller than the females. When a male finds a female in the depths, he bites the female to attach himself to her. The two remain attached for the rest of their lives.

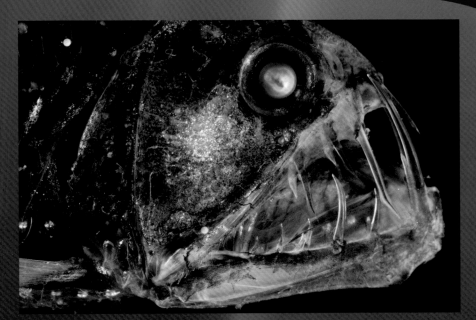

Viperfish are long, thin, eel-like fish. Their mouths are filled with teeth so sharp and long that they can't close their mouths! Viperfish have bioluminescent spots on their bodies. These spots draw prey to them.

OCEAN HABITATS QUIZ

1. **What causes the sea level to rise and fall?**

   a) The Earth's revolution
   b) The moon's gravity
   c) The sun's gravity
   d) The Earth's rotation

2. **Which animal does NOT live in a tide pool?**

   a) Sea urchin
   b) Coral polyp
   c) Sea star
   d) Crabs

3. **Which animal is NOT a mammal?**

   a) Tiger shark
   b) Blue whale
   c) Orca
   d) Dolphin

4. **How much of the Earth's surface is coral reef?**

   a) Less than 1 percent
   b) 10 percent
   c) 1 percent
   d) 25 percent

5. **Which fish lives among sea anemones?**

a) Pufferfish
b) Parrot fish
c) Lionfish
d) Clownfish

6. **Which animal lives in the Antarctic?**

a) Narwhal
b) Walrus
c) Polar bear
d) Emperor penguin

7. **Which animal migrates to lay its eggs?**

a) Dolphins
b) Whales
c) Sea turtles
d) Sharks

8. **What do fish use to breathe?**

a) Gills
b) Their mouth
c) Scales
d) They must swim to the surface to breathe

Answers: 1) b 2) b 3) a 4) a 5) d 6) d 7) c 8) a

GLOSSARY

Bioluminescence the shining of light from a living creature

Camouflage an animal's coloring that enables it to blend in with its surroundings

Currents flows of water in a specific direction and pattern within the ocean

Migrate to move long distances for food, to breed, or to lay eggs

Predator animal that hunts and eats other animals for food

Prey animals that are hunted by other animals for food

Sea level the surface level of the ocean halfway between low and high tide

Species a category of related living things that can interbreed

Tentacles long, flexible, armlike body parts on the head or around the mouth of some animals, used for grabbing and moving

Tide the rising and falling of the ocean surface that happens twice a day and is caused by the gravitational pull of the moon

ORCA

SEA URCHIN

TIGER SHARK

PUFFER FISH

OCTOPUS

WALRUS

Habitat: coral reefs, kelp forests, tide pools
Size: up to 10 inches wide
Diet: algae, kelp, seaweed

Sea urchins use both their tiny tube feet and their spines to move across the ocean floor.

Habitat: icy waters, open ocean
Size: up to 32 feet long, up to 6 tons
Diet: fish, seals, sea lions, squid, seabirds

Orcas have been known to fight and defeat great white sharks.

Habitat: coral reefs
Size: up to 3 feet long
Diet: algae, mussels, clams

Puffer fish can grow to two or three times their normal size when they puff up.

Habitat: open ocean
Size: up to 25 feet long, up to 1,900 pounds
Diet: stingrays, squid, birds, sea turtles, seals

These sharks get their name from the stripes on the bodies of young tiger sharks.

Habitat: icy waters
Size: up to 11½ feet long, up to 1½ tons
Diet: shellfish

A walrus relies on its sensitive whiskers to find shellfish on the seafloor.

Habitat: rocky shores
Size: up to 3 feet long
Diet: crabs, mollusks

Octopuses can change the color and texture of their skin to blend in with their surroundings.

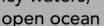

Smithsonian

FLIGHT

Stephen Binns

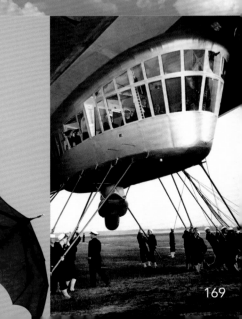

CONTENTS

READY FOR TAKEOFF!

Zoom!

The history of flight is a very short, very fast ride.
The secrets of flight were always there in the air for us to find.

When we did finally find them . . .

Zoom!

We were off! And we kept going faster and faster.
Welcome to the science of flight!
And welcome to a very short history of the very short history of flight!

BIRD FLIGHT

A pigeon can fly. A pig cannot fly. Well, of course. A pigeon is a bird. A pig is a mammal.
But a fruit bat can fly, while a kiwi cannot fly. The fruit bat is a mammal and the kiwi is a bird.

To fly on your own, you must be born with the gift for it. Every part of you must be built for flight.
The wings of the northern cardinal, unlike the wings of the kiwi, are long and wide enough to flap.

A flying bird flaps its wings up and down. A hummingbird does this fifty times a second.

It is a lot of very hard work, but birds have very light bones and very strong muscles to lift the bones.

Bats are the only mammals that are true fliers. They are built much like birds, though without feathers.

Feathers come in very handy, but they are not required for flight. Neither is flapping.

It took a long time for humans to figure this out.

Ancient people around the world knew that as air gets warmer, it rises. This is how a hot-air balloon rises.

The ancient Nazca people made giant line drawings on the plains of Peru that can only be seen from high above. How did they do it? An American researcher decided that they used a hot-air balloon.

In 1975, the researcher built a hot-air balloon using only materials that were part of Nazca life. The balloon was made of cloth and the balloon's basket was made of reeds. The balloon flew—with the researcher in it!

The researcher couldn't prove for sure that the Nazca people flew in hot air balloons. But he did prove that they could have.

In the history of human flight, there is a special place for the "tower jumpers" of the Middle Ages.

These pioneers of flight climbed to the highest place they could find. They put on feathered wings. They flapped their arms. They fell a long way to the ground. Historians of flight would call these flapping machines "ornithopters."

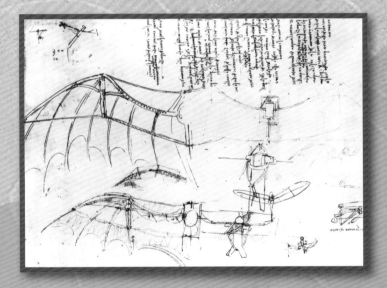

In the late 1400s, the famous artist and inventor Leonardo da Vinci made sketches for an ornithopter. Ropes and pulleys would help with the flapping. Modern **engineers** have built models based on Leonardo's idea.
But unlike the "Nazca balloon," Leonardo's flapping machine just doesn't work.

A manned balloon finally flew in 1783. The brothers Joseph and Étienne Montgolfier (eh-tee-YEN mon-GOLF-yay) launched their hot-air balloon with three passengers in the basket: a sheep, a rooster, and a duck.

The sheep was the first sheep to fly. The rooster and the duck were the first poultry to fly 1,500 feet above the earth.

A huge crowd gathered in Paris for the brothers' first manned launch of the balloon. Pilatre de Rozier became the first human in history to fly, though the balloon was tethered to the ground with an 80-foot rope. Later, Rozier and the Marquis d'Arlandes volunteered to go up in the balloon without the safety of the rope. It was the first true manned flight in history.

Benjamin Franklin was in Paris at the time and he saw it fly. A man near Franklin asked, "But what use is it?" Franklin replied, "Of what use is a new-born babe?"

The balloon was something new in the world. Benjamin Franklin, statesman and inventor, just wanted to see the show.

Meanwhile, a French inventor named Jacques Charles was at work on his own experiments in flight. Charles filled a giant cloth balloon with hydrogen, a gas lighter than air. The hydrogen caused the balloon to rise up into the sky.

The unmanned balloon flew off in the direction of a little village. The people of the village had heard nothing about the balloon and its launch. When the balloon landed, the villagers stabbed it with pitchforks.

They thought it was a flying monster!

"But what use is it?" that man in the crowd had asked.

An answer came ten years later. During the French Revolution, balloons were used to spy on the enemy from high in the sky.

THE GLIDER

A German engineer named Otto Lilienthal (LIL-yen-thal) took the next big step in flight. He was the first to go on a long flight controlled by the pilot. He invented the hang glider.

As children, Otto and his brother Gustav studied birds. They tried to fly with strapped-on wings. As an adult, Otto began to study birds that glide as well as flap. He put aside the idea of flapping.

Instead, he built fixed wings— wings that stay outstretched like the wings of a hawk as it glides. He tested the wings by launching himself from a little hill.

In 1894, Otto Lilienthal began launching himself on glides of 150 feet. He then moved to higher hills and flew 1,500 feet.

On August 9, 1896, Otto Lilienthal went to the hills to test a new glider. On his fourth flight, a gust of wind made the glider rise suddenly. He tried to push against this **turbulence**, but the glider stalled. He fell frity-nine feet and died the next day.

His brother Gustav reported his last words: "Sacrifices must be made."

Across the ocean, another pair of brothers read about Otto Lilienthal's death. They soon sent a letter to the Smithsonian in Washington, D.C., asking for information on human flight. It was then that their life's work began. Their names were Orville and Wilbur Wright.

The Wright brothers were bicycle builders in Ohio. In less than five years, they would become the first true masters of the air. On December 17, 1903, they launched an airplane with a motor that flew for twelve seconds.

The Wrights chose the beaches of Kitty Hawk, North Carolina, as the place to test their ideas. They learned that Kitty Hawk often had winds of a speed that Otto Lilienthal found best for his glider—between 15 and 20 miles an hour. Kitty Hawk also had high hills without trees and lots of sand for soft landings.

The Wrights first tested kites, then gliders. At home in Ohio, they built a **wind tunnel** out of a wooden box. A fan at one end of the box blew a stream of air against little model wings. They could test model wings of many different shapes and sizes.

Their 1903 motorized Wright Flyer was very much like the gliders they were testing. But it was larger and sturdier to hold the weight of the motor and two propellers at the back of the plane.

It was Orville who made the historic 12-second flight, then the brothers took turns. On the fourth flight of the day, Wilbur stayed in the air for about a minute—almost five times longer than the first flight.

WHAT THE WRIGHTS DID RIGHT

The Wright Flyer, like all planes today, set in motion the four forces of flight.

To fly, we must overcome the force of **gravity**. We overcome gravity with the force of **lift**. To lift, we must move forward through the air with the force of **thrust**. Air works against our thrust with the force of **drag.**

The Wright brothers found the right wing shape to lift the plane. Their wings—like bird wings and all airplane wings today—were shaped so that air must work harder to move over the top of the wing than under the bottom.

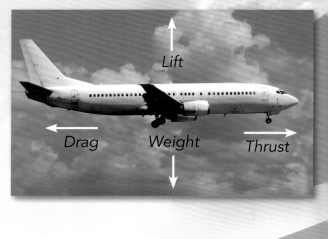

Lift

Drag　　Weight　　Thrust

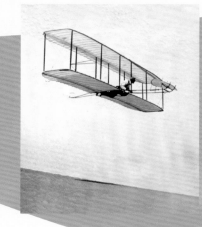

As it works to pass over the top of the wing, the air speeds up. When air speeds up, it loses pressure. The pressure on the top of the wings is then weaker than the pressure on the bottom of the wings. Every plane is held in the sky by the stronger pressure pushing on the bottom of the wings.

A bird gets both lift and thrust from its flapping wings. On an airplane, the forces are separate. Airplane wings do the work of lift. The airplane's engine system does the work of thrust.

The Wright brothers used a gasoline engine to power the two propellers. Propeller blades work like spinning wings. As they spin, there is a difference in pressure on the two sides of the blade. The plane is thrust forward by stronger pressure on the back of the blade.

Most large planes today are jets. A jet engine creates the thrust (like a propeller engine) and also creates the thrust (like the propeller itself). All of this happens inside the engine.

The Wright brothers invented ways of controlling and balancing a glider—better ways than Otto Lilienthal had found. For inspiration, they looked to the birds.

Wilbur Wright watched how a buzzard makes turns in the air. He saw that the bird twists one wingtip up and twists the other wingtip down.

One day he was talking to a customer in the bicycle shop. He was holding a small empty cardboard box in his hands. Without thinking about it, he pressed down on two opposite corners of the box. The other two corners moved. One went up and one went down.

He imagined the box as a span of wings. He saw that a plane's wingtips could be twisted this way to turn the plane, maybe by a system of wires.

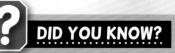
This simple motion is part of an airplane's flight. The plane's two ailerons move in opposite directions (one up, one down) to control the plane's **roll**.

Rudder   Wing

Elevator   Aileron

Look at the modern jet and look again at the Wright Flyer. There at the back of the Wright Flyer is a rudder to control **yaw**, or side-to-side motion.

Rudder

Wings

Elevator   Controls

There in the front is an elevator to control **pitch**, or up-and-down motion. But on the Wright Flyer, the elevator is at the front of the aircraft. Most aircraft have the elevator at the rear of the aircraft.

The Wrights' basic ideas carried the history of flight through the propeller years and into the jet age.

1908 Wilbur Wright travels to France for the first public showing of the Wright Flyer. He stays in the air for two and a half hours.

1914 A French airplane is the first to shoot down another airplane in World War I.

1919 British pilots John Alcock and Arthur Brown fly nonstop across the Atlantic.

1927 American Charles Lindbergh becomes the world's most famous pilot by flying nonstop across the Atlantic alone. He flies from New York to Paris in thirty-three hours.

1931 U.S. pilots Clyde Pangborn and Hugh Herndon fly nonstop across the Pacific, from Japan to Washington state, in forty-one hours.

1932 U.S. pilot Amelia Earhart is the first woman to make a solo nonstop flight across the Atlantic. Five years later, she disappears in the Pacific on a round-the-world flight.

1933 U.S. pilot Wiley Post makes a solo around-the-world flight (with stops) in seven days.

1936 The two-engine Douglas DC-3 passenger plane begins flying. It holds twenty-one passengers and flies at 200 miles an hour.

1941 America enters World War II when 353 Japanese fighter, bomber, and torpedo planes attack the U.S. naval base at Pearl Harbor, Hawaii.

1943 Franklin D. Roosevelt becomes the first U.S. president to fly while still president. He flies to Morocco to meet World War II allies.

1945 American B-29 planes drop two atomic bombs on Japan, ending World War II.

1946 The Lockheed Constellation, or "Connie," flies passengers from New York to Los Angeles in eleven hours, with one stop.

1953 The DC-7 becomes the first passenger plane to fly nonstop from coast to coast in both directions. It makes the flight in less than eight hours.

THE JET AGE

1939 Germany flies the first jet-powered aircraft, the Heinkel He 178.

1947 U.S. pilot Chuck Yeager is first to reach Mach 1, the speed of sound, in a rocket plane.

1953 The North American F-100 Super Sabre becomes the first jet fighter to reach supersonic speed.

1958 The Boeing 707 becomes the first successful jet airliner. The jet engines and fuel tanks can carry the large plane across the Atlantic.

1962 The supersonic North American X-15 rocket plane climbs more than fifty miles above the earth. Pilot Robert H. White is the first to touch outer space in a plane.

1963 An X-15 plane flies faster than Mach 6 (six times the speed of sound).

1969 The first "jumbo jet" begins flying. The Boeing 747 can carry more than 400 passengers.

1976 The supersonic Concorde goes into service. It can fly from New York to Paris in less than four hours, beating Charles Lindbergh's time by about thirty hours.

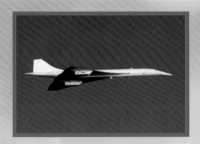

2003 The Concorde makes its last flight.

2005 American businessman Steve Fossett makes the first solo around-the-world flight without refueling. He travels from Salina, Kansas, to Salina, Kansas, in sixty-seven hours.

2007 The double-decker Airbus A380 becomes the world's largest jet airliner. It can carry more than 850 people.

ZOOM! BOOM!

Before the jet age could become the space age, scientists needed to figure out how manned aircraft could fly farther and faster.

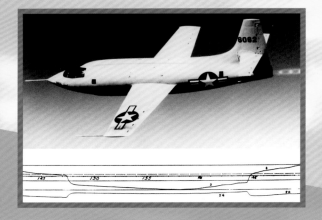

U.S. Air Force pilot Chuck Yeager broke the barrier on October 14, 1947, when he flew faster than the speed of sound, called Mach 1.

He made this first **supersonic** flight in a Bell X-1 rocket-engine plane. A rocket engine works a lot like a jet engine. But while a jet draws in oxygen from the air to burn fuel, a rocket carries its own liquid oxygen. A rocket is needed for travel into outer space, where there is no air.

The Bell X-1 was carried into the air in the belly of a B-29 bomber. The bomber dropped the X-1 as if it were a bomb. Then the plane shot like a rocket and climbed toward 40,000 feet. The speed of sound in that high thin air is 660 miles an hour.

Scientists thought that a plane breaking the sound barrier would make its own sound—a **sonic boom** loud enough to shatter glass down on the ground. But what would the speed do to the pilot?

Yeager's "machometer" showed him at .95 Mach and then .96 Mach and then . . .

Boom! People down on the ground in the California desert heard the sonic boom.

Yeager's plane shook but he was fine. He had broken the sound barrier at Mach 1.06 (700 miles an hour). This was just forty-four years after the Wright brothers' twelve-second flight.

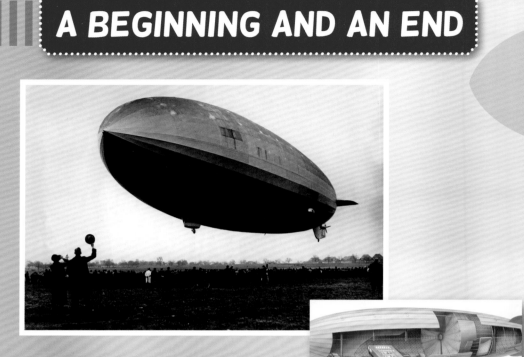

Travel by a craft lighter than air began with the Montgolfier balloon in the 1780s.

In the 1930s, lighter-than-air travel reached its peak and reached an end at the same time.

On May 3, 1937, the *Hindenburg* rose above Germany and floated over the Atlantic toward the United States. It was a German lighter-than-air dirigible, or airship. It had the comforts and luxuries of an ocean liner and it crossed the Atlantic in less than three days. That was half the time of an ocean liner.

The Hindenburg had sleeping cabins, a library, and even a piano lounge. The grand piano was made of light aluminum to save weight. A pianist could finish a performance and then lift the grand piano as an encore!

The *Hindenburg* was filled with hydrogen, the gas that Jacques Charles had used for his balloon. Hydrogen catches fire easily. On May 6, the *Hindenburg* caught fire and exploded as it was landing in New Jersey.

With that, the days of the airship were over.

But airplane travel in the United States was once a great luxury, too. Riding on a plane was a very big deal. A man always wore a tie on a plane. A woman might wear a hat and white gloves. People dressed for a flight as if going out to a nice restaurant.

And why not? Airline meal service, even on short flights, included full meals. And passengers ate it with real forks and knives!

The Boeing 747, the first "jumbo jet," began flying in 1970. Some 747s had spiral staircases between levels. And some even had a piano lounge, just like the *Hindenburg*.

The supersonic Concorde was a marvel, but not enough people were willing to pay for the ride. Very high costs of flying the plane meant very high airfares.

? DID YOU KNOW?

The Concorde is now only a museum piece. Air France donated one of the last Concordes to the Smithsonian in 2003.

Why don't we fly in such comfort and luxury today? Where did all the pianos go?

We still fly by the force of lift. We still move forward with the force of thrust.

But why has it all become such a drag?

Before 1978, the U.S. government set many rules, or regulations, that helped a few big airlines. The Airline Deregulation Act of 1978 led to more airlines and more competition. Airlines competed with lower prices rather than more comfort.

More and more people began to fly. Airlines packed more and more people into the planes.

The next time you fly, try taking the window seat, and look out the window and think about the marvel of flight.

For thousands of years, people built and engineered and invented, but they never reached the skies. They never saw the earth as you are seeing it from the window seat, though they dreamed about it all the time.

Then advances in flight came so fast that flying left the rest of the world behind.

It all took a lot of work and courage and genius. And many sacrifices were made.

1. **What invention's first passengers were a sheep, a rooster, and a duck?**

   a) An ornithopter
   b) A hot-air balloon
   c) A glider
   d) An airship

2. **What were Orville and Wilbur Wright's original jobs?**

   a) Glider builders
   b) Kite makers
   c) Bicycle builders
   d) Auto mechanics

3. **Who launched the first motorized airplane in 1903?**

   a) Jacques Charles
   b) Leonardo da Vinci
   c) Benjamin Franklin
   d) Wright brothers

4. **Which is NOT a force of flight?**

   a) Thrust
   b) Gravity
   c) Speed
   d) Drag

5. **Who flew faster than the speed of sound in 1947?**

a) Chuck Yeager
b) The Wright brothers
c) Amelia Earhart
d) Charles Lindbergh

6. **What does "supersonic" mean?**

a) Faster than the speed of sound
b) Rocket-powered
c) Sound barrier
d) Super hearing

7. **What was the *Hindenburg*?**

a) A rocket ship
b) A hot air balloon
c) An airship
d) An airplane

8. **How long did it take the Concorde to fly across the Atlantic Ocean?**

a) Twenty hours
b) Eight hours
c) Fourteen hours
d) Four hours

Answers: 1) b 2) c 3) d 4) c 5) a 6) a 7) c 8) d

GLOSSARY

Drag the force that slows down an aircraft's forward motion because of air resistance

Engineers people who design or build things based on science

Gravity the force that pulls an object toward the center of the Earth or another object that has mass

Lift an upward force caused by a vacuum above

Pitch the angle at which an airplane's nose points up or down as it rises or dives

Roll the movement of a plane as it leans toward one wing

Sonic boom a loud explosive sound caused by the shock wave from an aircraft traveling faster than the speed of sound

Supersonic faster than the speed of sound

Thrust the forward force created by a powerful source such as a propeller or jet engine

Turbulence unsteady movement caused by sudden changes in the speed or direction of the wind

Wind tunnel a device used to study the flow of air and its effect on objects

Yaw the side-to-side motion controlled by the rudder on the tail of a plane